Iran
The Nuclear Challenge

COUNCIL *on* **FOREIGN RELATIONS**

Elliott Abrams, Robert D. Blackwill, Robert M. Danin, Richard A. Falkenrath, Matthew Kroenig, Meghan L. O'Sullivan, and Ray Takeyh

Edited by Robert D. Blackwill

Iran
The Nuclear Challenge

The Council on Foreign Relations (CFR) is an independent, nonpartisan membership organization, think tank, and publisher dedicated to being a resource for its members, government officials, business executives, journalists, educators and students, civic and religious leaders, and other interested citizens in order to help them better understand the world and the foreign policy choices facing the United States and other countries. Founded in 1921, CFR carries out its mission by maintaining a diverse membership, with special programs to promote interest and develop expertise in the next generation of foreign policy leaders; convening meetings at its headquarters in New York and in Washington, DC, and other cities where senior government officials, members of Congress, global leaders, and prominent thinkers come together with CFR members to discuss and debate major international issues; supporting a Studies Program that fosters independent research, enabling CFR scholars to produce articles, reports, and books and hold roundtables that analyze foreign policy issues and make concrete policy recommendations; publishing *Foreign Affairs*, the preeminent journal on international affairs and U.S. foreign policy; sponsoring Independent Task Forces that produce reports with both findings and policy prescriptions on the most important foreign policy topics; and providing up-to-date information and analysis about world events and American foreign policy on its website, CFR.org.

The Council on Foreign Relations takes no institutional positions on policy issues and has no affiliation with the U.S. government. All views expressed in its publications and on its website are the sole responsibility of the author or authors.

For further information about CFR or this publication, please write to the Council on Foreign Relations, 58 East 68th Street, New York, NY 10065, or call Communications at 212.434.9888. Visit CFR's website, www.cfr.org.

Contents

Foreword

Richard N. Haass

"Foreign policy is hard" was one of my refrains when I taught the subject decades ago to aspiring policymakers at Harvard's John F. Kennedy School of Government. Nothing has emerged in the intervening years to make it any less daunting. To the contrary, the emergence of new actors, forces, and technologies has if anything added to the difficulty of understanding what is going on in the world and deciding what to do about it.

The subject of Iran's nuclear ambitions turns out to be particularly hard. This is the case at every level: the descriptive, the analytical, and the prescriptive. Each is worth considering here, albeit briefly.

Simply presenting what is known as opposed to being uncertain is challenging, in part because Iran is going to considerable lengths to make it difficult for outsiders to be certain about what it is actually doing in the nuclear realm. We are often reduced to estimates of those activities and facilities that are acknowledged—and have little or no information about what is taking place at undeclared, concealed facilities.

Even more difficult to discern are intentions, especially when it comes to a government of multiple, often competing centers of power. Have Iranian leaders decided to build nuclear weapons and, if so, how many? Have they decided to stop just short of crossing the weapons threshold? Are they prepared to accept a ceiling on their nuclear activities that would preclude nearing the weapons threshold? The questions are virtually unlimited. Foreign policy is carried out almost always with incomplete and inaccurate information; here the degree of inaccuracy and incompleteness is greater than is the norm.

Analysis is no easier. What impact are sanctions having and likely to have on Iranian decision-making? How would Iran's behavior change if it did come to possess one or more nuclear weapons? Would Iran's leaders be susceptible to the same logic of deterrence as others appear to have been or are? Would they ever transfer material or weapons to third parties? Would they ever threaten to use or actually use a nuclear weapon? If so, under what circumstances? How would Iran's neighbors react to its emergence as a state with nuclear weapons? What might be done and with what effect to change their calculations? Again, there are far more questions than answers.

Not surprisingly, prescribing what to do either to prevent Iran from acquiring near or actual weapons status or to contend with it if it does is exceedingly complex. There are drawbacks, including both sizable costs and risks, associated with any and every course of action. But complexity and opacity cannot justify avoiding the problem. Not reaching a conclusion and not acting are as consequential a policy as anything else.

This volume is designed to assess the tools and strategies associated with the challenge posed by Iran and its nuclear program. The essays in this volume thus discuss the contours of Iran's nuclear program, the use of sanctions and their possible effect, the potential for a negotiated settlement, the consequences of both Israeli and American military action, the prospects for regime change, and policies that should be considered if for one reason or another policymakers are confronted with the need to cope with an actual or near Iranian nuclear weapons capability.

The essays are all written by individuals associated with the David Rockefeller Studies Program of the Council on Foreign Relations. Each has strong views about the Iran situation and what should be done about it. Each, however, has held back and instead produced an essay that illuminates the challenges and potential policy choices.

The result is a book that chooses not to argue for a particular analysis or a particular course of action. Rather, the purpose of this collection of essays is to help the reader understand the parameters of Iran's nuclear program, the policy choices available to the United States and others, and their potential consequences. The aim of this volume is not to tell the reader *what* to think but rather *how* to think about Iran's nuclear activities and the options for addressing them.

As a result, the volume is entirely consistent with the mission of CFR, which is to be "a resource for its members, government officials, business executives, journalists, educators and students, civic and religious leaders, and other interested citizens in order to help them better understand the world and the foreign policy choices facing the United States and other countries." It is also consistent with the tradition that the organization takes no collective position on matters of policy.

I want to thank the authors—Elliott Abrams, Robert D. Blackwill, Robert M. Danin, Richard A. Falkenrath, Matthew Kroenig, Meghan L. O'Sullivan, and Ray Takeyh—for their written contributions as well as for the time and effort put into reacting to the drafts of one another. This was and is a collaborative effort in every sense.

I want to express special thanks to Bob Blackwill, who helped both conceive this volume and bring it to fruition as its editor. His concluding chapter, which ends with questions rather than answers, captures the spirit of this project.

I also want to thank James M. Lindsay, senior vice president and director of studies, for his involvement with this effort from its commencement. The intellectual strength and diversity of this volume's contributors are a testament to the quality of CFR's in-house think tank under Jim's leadership. My thanks also to Patricia Dorff, CFR's editorial director, for all she did to ensure this book's timely release, and Kathryn Sparks, Ambassador Blackwill's research associate, for her able administrative support.

What give this project and its product extra significance are the stakes. They are great by any measure. What is done and not done by the United States and others, what is averted, and what comes to be will have enormous consequences for the world economy, the future of the global nuclear nonproliferation regime, and the trajectory of the greater Middle East. This region has more often than not been defined by conflict more than peace, by instability more than order, and by repression more than freedom. What happens to and with Iran and its nuclear program will meaningfully affect the next chapter of this region and through it the world.

Maps

IRAN'S NUCLEAR SITES

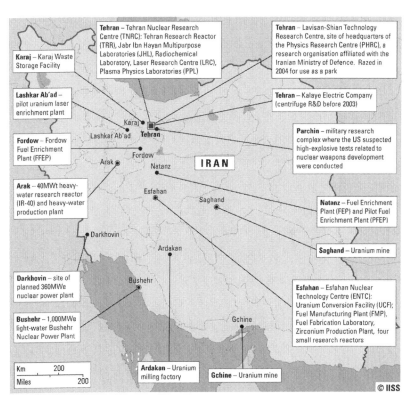

"Map: Iran's Nuclear facilities," *Iran's Nuclear, Chemical and Biological Capabilities: A net assessment,* © The International Institute for Strategic Studies, February 3, 2011, p. 50. Reprinted with permission.

IRAN IN THE REGION

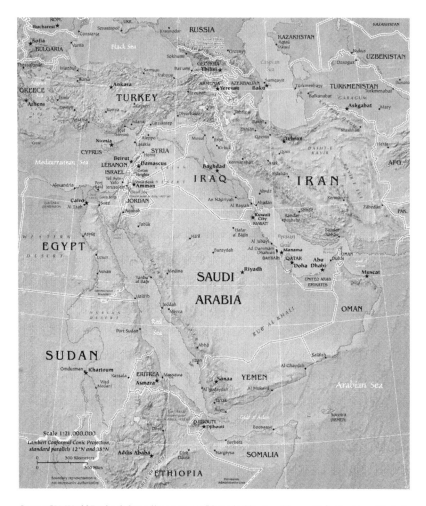

Source: CIA World Factbook, https://www.cia.gov/library/publications/the-world-factbook/graphics/ref_maps/pdf/middle_east.pdf.

Introduction: What Do We Know?

Ray Takeyh

At present, Iran can best be described as a country determined to pre-serve for itself the option of acquiring nuclear weapons capability at some future date: to shorten, to the greatest extent possible, the time it will take to build these weapons (and to warn the world) once the decision is made to do so, by developing dispersed, hardened dual-use nuclear fuel cycle capabilities; and to seek shelter from international nonproliferation pressure in the Nuclear Nonproliferation Treaty's (NPT) promise of access to nuclear technology for peaceful purposes.

In chronological form, the basic contours of the Iranian nuclear pro-gram are as follows:

- In the mid-1980s, the Khomeini regime secretly decided to restart a nuclear program, including preparatory work for the acquisition of a nuclear weapon, that had begun under the shah. This decision is believed to have been influenced by the devastation inflicted on Iran by Iraq's use of chemical weapons during the Iran-Iraq War.

- From about 1990 on, Iran worked to develop its own nuclear fuel cycle infrastructure—uranium mining, conversion, and enrichment—and heavy-water production for a heavy-water reactor for the production of plutonium. In the mid-1990s, Iran began to secretly purchase and take delivery of uranium enrichment centrifuges from the A. Q. Khan network.[1] Iran began to test these centrifuges in 2000.

- In 2001, Iran began to construct its main enrichment facility in Natanz, approximately two hundred miles south of Tehran. The plant is constructed to eventually accommodate fifty thousand cen-trifuges, giving Iran the ability to produce massive quantities of enriched uranium.

- In 2002, secret Iranian fuel cycle activities were publicly revealed, fundamentally changing the diplomatic landscape. From this point on, Britain, France, and Germany (the EU3) and the International

Atomic Energy Agency (IAEA) began to play much more significant roles in the diplomatic effort to address the problem. The IAEA conducted limited inspections of Iran's previously clandestine facilities and discovered additional evidence of Iran's concealment of undeclared fuel cycle activities.[2]

 – In late 2003, the EU3 persuaded the government of President Mohammad Khatami to suspend its enrichment program and accept the NPT Additional Protocol.[3] Furthermore, the U.S. intelligence community assessed that, in the fall of 2003, the Iranian government halted its clandestine research and development program for nuclear weapons—but not the nuclear fuel cycle systems, such as centrifuges, needed to produce the fissile material for a possible weapon. (British intelligence services surveying the same information concluded that though Iran halted weaponization activities in 2003, it subsequently resumed them.) In sum, the circumstantial evidence strongly suggests that Iran is, at a minimum, aiming to develop a nuclear weapons capability. The U.S. military presence in Afghanistan, on Iran's eastern border, and in Iraq, on Iran's western border, was presumably a factor in Iran's 2003–2004 nuclear decision-making.

 – The EU3's agreement with the Iranian government collapsed after the election of Mahmoud Ahmadinejad in 2005.

 – In 2009, the government of Iran disclosed to the IAEA the existence of a new uranium enrichment facility at Fordow, outside Qom; this facility had already been detected by Western intelligence. The IAEA believes that enrichment operations began there in December 2011, that the facility's purpose is to enrich uranium beyond the 5 percent U-235 concentration achieved at Natanz, and that it is undergoing construction designed to further expand its capacity to eventually accommodate more than three thousand centrifuges. The Fordow facility is better protected than the Natanz facility and thus less susceptible to destruction by air or missile strikes.

Since 2007, U.S. intelligence services have asserted that no evidence suggests that Supreme Leader Ali Khamenei has made the final decision to construct nuclear weapons, but it is clear that he is accumulating the necessary resources and technologies that will provide him with that option. "They are certainly moving on that path, but we don't believe that they have actually made the decision to go ahead with a nuclear weapon," stressed James Clapper, the director of National Intelligence, in his testimony to the Senate Select Committee on Intelligence in February 2012.[4] Although the acquisition of these fuel cycle capabilities could be justified under the same legal theory that Iran is entitled to the benefits of nuclear technology for civil, peaceful purposes, Iran elected to carry out this work secretly and often in violation of its nuclear safeguards commitments to the IAEA.

THE DIPLOMATIC CONTEXT: THE 1990S AND BUSHEHR

The United States has been attempting to stop or at least delay the Iranian nuclear problem since at least the mid-1990s, when Iran contracted with the Russian Ministry for Atomic Energy to complete the construction of the pressurized water reactor nuclear power plant at Bushehr. A German firm began, but did not complete, the construction of the Bushehr complex in 1975, and the reactors had been damaged during the Iran-Iraq War.

The construction of the Bushehr reactor complex was the most visible element of the Iranian nuclear program, and the Clinton administration focused its diplomacy on attempting to dissuade the Russian government from providing nuclear assistance to Iran. The administration was partially successful: it persuaded Russia to not provide the uranium enrichment technology and heavy-water reactor also sought by Iran, and to both supply and retrieve the nuclear fuel that would eventually power the Bushehr reactors.

The Clinton administration's diplomacy toward the Iranian nuclear program had two critical handicaps. The first was that, at the time, Iran was in good standing as a nonnuclear weapons state party to the 1968 Nuclear Nonproliferation Treaty. The central bargain in the NPT is that the nonnuclear weapons states party to the treaty foreswear the acquisition of nuclear weapons; in return, they are guaranteed access to nuclear technology for peaceful purposes. In the mid-1990s, as it does today, Iran argued that it had an international legal right to benefit from civil nuclear power, as many other nations have. In a formal legal sense, the Clinton administration's opposition to the sale of nuclear technology to Iran turned on its assertion that Iran had a covert nuclear weapons program, and therefore was not in good standing with the NPT and not entitled to unbridled access to technology that would accelerate its ability to break out of its NPT commitments. This argument worked reasonably well in Washington and Tel Aviv, but the United States could not prove its case to the rest of the world.

Thus the second handicap had to do with the intelligence on the Iranian nuclear weapons program. In the mid-1990s, the U.S. intelligence community suspected the existence of a covert nuclear weapons program in Iran, but the evidence was almost entirely circumstantial, highly classified, or both. This made it next to impossible to rally broad-based international support around a diplomatic effort to stop Iran's program, or even to talk constructively with the Iranian government about the matter.

Today, unlike the 1990s, there is extensive direct evidence of Iranian efforts to deceive the international community, in violation of its NPT and IAEA safeguards agreements, about its development of dual-use nuclear fuel cycle capabilities. Any concrete information regarding whether Iran has made efforts to construct nuclear weapons ("weaponize") is not publicly available.

The Bushehr reactors began operation under IAEA safeguards in 2010. In part because of the success of U.S. diplomacy toward Iran's chief nuclear supplier (Russia), the direct contribution of Bushehr to the Iranian nuclear weapons program is modest because there is no way that any significant quantity of weapons-usable fissile material can be diverted from Bushehr without several years' notice to the international community.

In addition to Bushehr, Iran has declared fourteen nuclear facilities and nine locations outside those installations where nuclear research is being conducted pursuant to its safeguard obligations to the IAEA. For instance, the latest IAEA report suggests that Natanz contains 54 installed cascades amounting to 9,156 centrifuges. Not all of these cascades are operational; as a result, 8,088 centrifuges were being fed nuclear fuel for enrichment purposes. The same report also states that Iran has 5,451 kilograms of enriched uranium at below 5 percent level in hand. (All the centrifuges at this installation are the more primitive IR-1 models, but Iran is known to have experimented with more advanced machines.)

Although it is clear that Iran has focused on uranium enrichment as the mainstay of its fissile material production capability, it has not neglected plutonium—the other fissile material commonly used in nuclear weapons—paths to nuclear empowerment. The heavy-water facilities in Esfahan and the nearly completed plant in Arak point to the fact that Iran's plutonium capabilities are also advancing. Although much of the focus of the international community is on Iran's growing enrichment capabilities, Tehran has attempted to diversify its nuclear portfolio, giving its leaders multiple avenues to achieve a nuclear weapons capability if they elect to do so.

WEAPONIZATION TIMETABLE

The question of how long it will take the Islamic Republic to assemble a weapon, if it decides to do so, is at the core of the present international crisis.

The weaponization timetable question is extremely complex and includes extensive technical uncertainties. U.S. intelligence assessments of this question are highly classified, drawing on not just sensitive sources and methods but also the U.S. government's own nuclear weapons expertise.

Before offering an assessment of the Iranian weaponization timetable, two essential framing points should be made.

First, every country has the potential to become a nuclear weapons state. Some countries—Japan, for example—would have a short timetable because of advanced civil nuclear facilities. Other countries such as Saudi Arabia, Egypt, Brazil, Australia, and Nigeria lack the same civil nuclear capacity and so would have a much longer road to travel, but they could certainly get there eventually. Iran lies somewhere in the middle.

The laws of physics, the distribution of natural resources and of basic scientific information, and the efficiency of global commerce rule out the possibility of precluding any determined state's eventual acquisition of nuclear weapons. The appropriate metric for judging nonproliferation and disarmament agreements is thus not whether they eliminate a country's option of acquiring nuclear weapons, which is impossible, but instead the time they reliably extend a country's weaponization timetable.

Second, when countries build nuclear weapons, they have a wide range of design decisions to make, and these decisions will determine not just when they will have a nuclear weapons capability but also what that capability will be. These decisions include, but are by no means limited to

 – whether to optimize centrifuge operations for material conservation (ratio of feed uranium to unit of enrichment), cost efficiency (operating costs of centrifuges), maximizing production of particular quantities for particular enrichment levels, material purity, or any other technical parameter inherent in an enrichment cascade;
 – whether the feedstock fed into an enrichment cascade is natural uranium (0.7 percent U-235) or partially enriched (1 to 20 percent U-235), as partially enriched uranium can be increased to highly enriched uranium (90 percent U-235) more quickly and with less energy and natural uranium;
 – how to optimize weapons design for material efficiency (allowing more weapons for a given quantity of fissile material), reliability (generally allowing fewer but less efficient weapons), safety, weight, yield, and use control;
 – whether to conduct weaponization work in secret or in a manner that provides obvious internationally observable indicators (such as expelling IAEA inspectors and diverting material from safeguarded facilities);
 – whether to rely on designs derived from foreign sources or publicly available data, or to indigenously develop new designs;
 – whether to produce abroad or fabricate internally the nonfissile components of the weapon;
 – whether to develop nuclear weapons delivery systems simultaneously or sequentially with weapons development;
 – whether to design weapons to withstand the physical stresses of ballistic reentry or the lesser ones of air or conventional delivery;
 – how tightly to compartmentalize the weapons development program, and how to recruit, train, and manage the technical personnel needed to work within it;
 – how many weapons to attempt to acquire, and over what time period (that is, whether to acquire a small number as quickly as possible, or build a larger arsenal steadily); and
 – whether and how to test the weapons and weapon delivery systems.

The historical record now offers about two dozen examples of countries that have developed nuclear weapons, have considered doing so, or are doing so currently. Despite the many unknowns and uncertainties, what is quite clear is that no two countries do it precisely the same way. Each makes decisions based on its capabilities, strategic context, internal politics, and learning from others.

Thus, in considering the Iranian weaponization timetable, the important issues are the assumptions about what the Iranian nuclear weapons objectives are and how the Iranian government will go about designing and building its nuclear weapons capability.

If one assumes that Iran aspires to have only a few testable nuclear weapons but to have them as soon as possible, then it is logical to also assume that it will optimize its centrifuge cascade to maximize the production of highly enriched uranium (HEU); opt for a weapons design that is simple and reliable, but not highly efficient from a material conservation or a military deployment perspective; and carry out all these activities simultaneously. Such a weapon would more likely be kept in a laboratory than given to operational units. Nongovernment experts believe that if Iran made the decision to enrich to a higher level today, it could produce enough weapons-grade uranium for one bomb in four months.[5] The same experts estimate that by the end of 2012 the time might be as little as one month.[6] However, this would require Iran to use its safeguarded facilities, a development unlikely to escape detection. Extrapolating from these estimates leads to public estimates that it would take Iran about a year to produce such a nuclear weapon if it decided to do so.[7] After it has this basic weapons capability, Iran would have to continue the long, difficult development process of producing more fissile material, modifying its weapons designs to make them more useful and efficient, and figuring out how to deploy the weapons on delivery systems, making them militarily useful.

But the timetable is entirely different if one assumes that the government of Iran has a longer time frame and more extensive nuclear ambitions. Say, for example, that Iran aspires not to have a few weapons in a laboratory next year but instead one hundred weapons fielded, mated with delivery vehicles, and deployed in the field within a decade. In that case, the timetable would of course be much longer and, most important, the various technical tasks—construction of production and storage facilities, installation and testing of fissile material production systems, procurement of raw materials and technical components, production of fissile material, management of waste products, recruitment and training of technical personnel, design of weapons, construction of weapons, testing of weapons, integration of weapons with delivery systems, and so on—would be carried out more sequentially and deliberately than in the rapid breakout scenario.

Building a nuclear weapon requires a state to perform a wide range of discrete, complex technical tasks, and then to integrate the output of these tasks coherently and logically. The tasks can be done simultaneously—which is generally more difficult and error prone—or sequentially. For this reason, a decision to delay progress in a particular aspect of a nuclear weapons program does not necessarily delay achievement of a state's overall strategic objectives in its desired time frame; in some cases, delay in one area may even help by allowing time, and freeing resources, for the other areas to catch up.

This point is central to the nonproliferation value of a diplomatic outcome that suspends only a particular aspect of Iran's current enrichment operations. Depending on one's assumptions of Iran's strategic objectives, such an outcome may have no impact whatsoever on when Iran achieves the nuclear weapons capability it wants—that is, it will not reliably extend the weaponization timetable and might even help Iran.

THE INTERNAL CONTEXT: IRAN'S POLITICS AND DELIBERATIONS

At a government level, for the past seven years there is no question that President Ahmadinejad has framed the nuclear issue as a matter of national sovereignty and greatness, and that the resistance of international pressure to curtail the nuclear program has become, if not the raison d'être, then at least a pillar of the struggling Islamic republic. The roots of this Iranian position are complex but clearly relate to Iran's difficult strategic position, surrounded by dangerous neighbors; to Iran's unique identity as the custodian of an ancient, great Persian nation and the center of Shia Islam; and to Iran's fragmented domestic politics.

The trajectory of Iran's nuclear program suggests that it rests on a more formidable scientific infrastructure than often assumed. Iran, in many ways, is an outlier in the history of proliferation: nearly every middle power that has obtained the bomb has had substantial assistance from an external patron. China acquired from the Soviet Union not just technical advice but also the means of building a nuclear reactor, weapon designs, and a supply of ballistic missiles. China in turn provided Pakistan enough enriched uranium for two bombs, helped with the construction of its enrichment facility and plutonium reactors, and furnished bomb designs. Israel received from France a nuclear reactor, underground plutonium reprocessing plant, and weapon designs. India, which has long claimed its nuclear program as an indigenous accomplishment, conveniently leaves out the fact that it received a nuclear reactor from Canada and twenty tons of heavy water from the United States. Isolated and ostracized, South Africa comes closest to Iran's predicament, in that it had to rely on internal resources for constructing the bomb, but it did receive tritium, which is critical for the explosion of thermonuclear weapons, from Israel.

Although Iran received Russian assistance in completing its light-water reactor, which is difficult to misuse for weapons purposes, and, ominously, rudimentary centrifuges from the A. Q. Khan network, Tehran never enjoyed the type of external patronage that other proliferators garnered. Moreover, no state has confronted such systematic attempts to disrupt its nuclear program through technology denial and computer virus penetration. That Iran has crossed successive technical thresholds, has managed to sustain an elaborate and growing enrichment network, and is working on a new generation of centrifuges are all indications of its scientific acumen.

What made this possible? The 1980s were a calamitous decade for science in Iran, as a revolutionary assault on the universities and the prolonged war with Iraq deprived the educational sector of funds and state support. But this changed in the 1990s, despite sanctions and export controls imposed on Iran after the 1979 revolution, as the political elites sought to revive scientific research. New organizations such as the Zanjan Institute for Advanced Studies in Basic Sciences and the Institute for Theoretical Physics and Mathematics were created; old institutions such as Sharif University of Technology were revived. The Atomic Energy Organization, which was protected by then speaker of the parliament Ayatollah Hashemi Rafsanjani even in the heady days of revolutionary turmoil, enjoyed a new management team and greater state allocations. The results have been impressive: the number of scientific papers produced by Iranian scholars in internationally recognized journals has increased dramatically, and many universities have enough resources and faculty expertise to offer their own doctoral programs.

Iran's scientists have emerged as strong nationalists determined to transcend factional politics and provide their country the full spectrum of technological discovery, including advances in nuclear science. Iran's pariah status has ironically engendered an esprit de corps within its scientific community. Researchers resent being shunned by their international colleagues, and are annoyed at being excluded from collaborative work with Western centers of learning that are crucial to scientific advancement. In today's Iran, rulers and scientists have crafted a national compact whereby the state provides the resources and the scientists furnish their expertise. A dedicated corps of scientific nationalists is committed to providing its country with the capacity to reach the heights of technological achievement.

All this is not to suggest that a change in Iranian government has not had a measurable impact on its strategic calculus. Given its protracted conflict with the United States, many in Iran consider the acquisition of nuclear weapons capability an important objective. The newspaper *Kayhan* openly called for acquiring "knowledge and ability to make nuclear weapons that are necessary in preparation for the next phase of the battlefield."[8] Ali Larijani, a leading figure in the Islamic Republic, has similarly stipulated that "if Iran becomes atomic Iran, no longer will anyone dare to challenge it because they would have to pay too high of a price."[9] Nuclear weapons may have been sought as tools of deterrence by previous Iranian regimes, but for many today they are a critical means of solidifying Iran's preeminence in the region. As such, a hegemonic Iran is assisted by a robust and extensive nuclear infrastructure.

The primary supporters and drivers of the nuclear program within the Iranian government are elements associated with Supreme Leader Ali Khamenei. Through command of central institutions, such as the Revolutionary Guards and the Guardian Council, they have enormous influence on national security planning. A fundamental tenet of their ideology is that the Islamic Republic is in constant danger from predatory external forces, necessitating military self-reliance. This perception was initially molded by a revolution that sought not just to defy international norms but also to refashion them. The passage of time and the failure of that mission have not necessarily diminished widespread suspicions of the international order and its primary guardian, the United States.

At the core, all disarmament agreements call on a state to forgo a certain degree of sovereignty in exchange for enhanced security. Once it renounces its weapons of mass destruction program, a state can be assured of support from the international community should it be threatened by another state possessing such arms. This implied trade-off has no value for many in Iran. Iran's prolonged war with Iraq has done much to condition the Iranian worldview and behavior. Iraq's use of chemical weapons against Iran—with impunity, if not tacit acceptance of Western powers—has reinforced Iran's suspicions of international order. For many within the Islamic Republic's leadership, the only way to safeguard Iran's interests is to develop an independent nuclear deterrent.

Beyond the legacy of the Iran-Iraq War, the international community's demand that Iran relinquish its fuel cycle capabilities has aroused the leadership's nationalistic impulses. Historically the subject of foreign intervention and the imposition of capitulation treaties, Iran is inordinately sensitive to its national prerogatives and sovereign rights. The rulers of Iran perceive that they are being challenged not because of their provocations and previous treaty violations, but because of superpower bullying. In a peculiar way, the nuclear program and Iran's national identity are fused in the imagination of many Iranians. To stand against the United States on this issue is to validate one's revolutionary ardor and sense of nationalism. Thus, the notion of compromise and acquiescence has limited utility to Iran's aggrieved nationalists.

The one issue that provokes a slight but perceptible disagreement within the governing bloc is the necessity of negotiations. Elements within the Revolutionary Guards dismiss diplomacy and suggest that Washington is not interested in proliferation but instead merely exploiting the nuclear issue to multilateralize its coercive policy. Given the immutable hostility of the United States to Iran, any concessions on the nuclear program would lead only to further impositions. Thus, they dismiss negotiations and call for Iran to press ahead with its activities regardless of international concerns and sensitivities.

The ultimate arbiter of Iranian politics and the person responsible for setting the national course remains Khamenei. Thus far Khamenei has found much to recommend in the Revolutionary Guard perception. He has echoed their claims in stressing that any "setback will encourage the enemy to become more assertive."[10] A supreme leader who has survived a myriad of internal challenges and the external threat of American intervention, he seems at ease with nuclear advocacy. Yet Khamenei cannot always afford bellicosity. He has accepted the importance of diplomatic engagement and has maintained Iran's basic commitment to the NPT. Thus far, the supreme leader has opted for a more judicious and incremental approach to nuclear empowerment. It is a strategy that has served him well as Iran has succeeded in expanding its nuclear infrastructure and has transgressed a series of Western red lines. The price for such advances has been increasing economic penalties and a degree of international isolation. How Khamenei balances the nuclear program with the economic well-being of his country and whether that calculus changes as Iran encounters financial distress will determine the nature of Iran's nuclear path.

The Role and Potential of Sanctions

Meghan L. O'Sullivan

American and international policymakers have placed their faith in economic sanctions as a tool that can resolve the current standoff with Iran
over its alleged pursuit of a nuclear weapon. Secretary of State Hillary
Clinton has spoken of "crippling sanctions" bringing Iran to the negotiating table; President Barack Obama has also outlined a vision in which
sanctions compel Iran to make concessions that allow for a diplomatic
solution. Even Israeli prime minister Benjamin Netanyahu has been
willing to give sanctions time in the hopes of resolving the looming
security problem with Iran without the use of military force.

The appeal of a sanctions-led solution is obvious. Sanctions offer
the possibility of achieving an acceptable outcome without military
force and its numerous uncertainties and unintended consequences.
The allure of sanctions is not new; American administrations back to
President Jimmy Carter have layered sanctions on Iran in the hopes of
achieving various and sundry goals—from gaining the release of U.S.
hostages in the wake of the Iranian revolution, to dissuading Iran from
supporting groups in violent opposition to Israel, to convincing Iran to
abandon efforts to develop a nuclear bomb.

Over the decades, the popularity of sanctions as a tool for addressing
Iran's problematic behavior has led to a byzantine array of sanctions.
Most extensive are U.S. sanctions, some of which date to 1979 and the
Iranian revolution. Many are intended to inhibit Iran's energy sector,
including "extraterritorial sanctions" first imposed on third parties and
other countries making energy investments in 1995 and more recently
expanded to cover refined products or the ability to create them. The
United States also precludes trade with and non-energy investment
in Iran, although a number of relatively small exemptions and excep-
tions are made in these areas. Most recent and perhaps most innovative
are the U.S. financial sanctions, which have sought to constrain Iran's
access to the international banking system: some target Iranian banks

directly, but the newest seek to penalize foreign banks that help the Iranian central bank process oil sales. In addition, a raft of U.S. sanctions are associated with Iran's designation as a state sponsor of terrorism and with the effort to keep weapons of mass destruction (WMD) technology from Iranian possession.

An ever-widening number of sanctions have also been imposed by non-U.S. countries and bodies. The United Nations (UN) has imposed sanctions on Iran related to WMD infrastructure, frozen the assets of individuals and banks associated with the Revolutionary Guard, and called for travel bans on designated individuals. Europe and other countries in the Organization for Economic Cooperation and Development (OECD) have put even more aggressive measures into place against Iran: in January 2012, the European Union agreed to discontinue the purchase of Iranian oil by July 1, 2012, and to freeze the assets of the Iranian Central Bank. Other countries, such as Japan, South Korea, and to a lesser extent India and Turkey, have sought to cut back on imports of Iranian oil, if only to avoid the extraterritorial sanctions that Congress has asked President Obama to place on those using the Iranian central bank for payments.

In the past, one might legitimately accuse some policymakers of turning to sanctions as a lowest common denominator, a means of responding to a perceived threat or advancing an interest when they were unable or unwilling to deploy other tools; policymakers were often willing to accept the low odds of success generally associated with sanctions. The use of sanctions on Iran today, however, has a distinctly different feel. Given the commitment of the United States and other countries to prevent Iran from acquiring nuclear weapons, the uncertain ability of sanctions to produce results in this case carries high stakes. Whereas in many other instances, the failure of sanctions would not instigate another course of action, a failure vis-à-vis Iran today could well prompt military action by Israel or the United States.

PROSPECTS FOR SANCTIONS' SUCCESS

What are the prospects that sanctions will succeed in contributing to the desired result? What is the likelihood that sanctions will create sufficient pressure to bring Iran to the negotiating table—not just to buy time or to split the coalition arrayed against it, but in a meaningful way?

Quite simply, will sanctions work? At different points in history, policymakers have envisioned a variety of ways in which sanctions could achieve sought-after outcomes—from regime change to containment. Today, as in the 1990s, the hope and desire is that sanctions will create enough pressure on the regime in Tehran to bring it to the negotiating table, ultimately compelling Iran to make the sorts of concessions regarding its nuclear program it has thus far resisted.

It is first important to acknowledge that sanctions almost never "work" when they make up the entirety of a strategy. They stand the best chance of working when they are strategically coupled with other foreign policy tools. In this instance, the necessary complementary instruments are both military force and negotiations. Sanctions in themselves are unlikely to lead Iran to abandon any nuclear pursuits. Sanctions in combination with the threat of military force and inducements in the form of possible carrots to be extended to a post-agreement Iran in the context of a diplomatic negotiation, which might enable a nonnuclear weapons Iran to save face, seem to be at least a plausible proposition.

The formula for such a sanctions-led strategy is not exact, and one can legitimately contest whether the threats of military force today are convincing, whether possible carrots are realistic, and whether negotiations are structured to maximize the chances of success. One might also underscore the importance of timing; given the lag between the imposition of sanctions and their impact, sanctions put in place years ago are likely to be more useful in undergirding a sanctions-based diplomatic solution embarked on today. That said, unlike in years past, when sanctions were relied on to carry the entire burden of U.S. policy, today's current sanctions regime is complemented by other instruments—positive and negative—that are at least more credible.

Moving away from the structural, consider whether the current sanctions will have an economic impact on Iran. Here, there is little debate: sanctions are already taking a significant toll on Iran's economy. Sales of oil are down markedly; Iran is having difficulty offloading oil; and it is facing a serious shortage of hard currency, resulting in a dramatic 40 percent plunge in the value of the rial from December 2011 to March 2012. Iran's oil production has fallen to a ten-year low of 3.38 million barrels per day (b/d). Although it is of course always difficult, if not impossible, to definitively separate out the effects of sanctions from those of Iran's poor economic policies and ill-thought-out strategies, Iranian officials themselves have stopped denying the economic impact of sanctions.

The impact of the sanctions on Iran today is the result of significant innovations in how sanctions are structured and used. For decades, a central maxim in the world of sanctions has been that if they are to have an impact, they need to be multilateral in a broad sense, if not universal. Comprehensive, aggressive U.S. sanctions on Iran throughout much of the 1990s and 2000s seemed to reinforce this notion; however, although they did create some economic discomfort for Iran, mostly by dampening its investment climate, the pain was relatively minor.

Sanctions against Iran in the past few years have turned globalization on its head. Opponents of unilateral or partial sanctions used to anticipate that such tools would grow more and more superfluous in a rapidly globalizing world, that they would only create a momentary irritation to the target before the global economy would rebalance its imports and exports. In practice, however, globalization has been a friend as well as a foe of sanctions. The "new generation" of financial sanctions on Iran have targeted the various nodes that connect Iran to the global economy; the more integrated Iran is into international financial markets, the more vulnerable it is to these sanctions.

Unfortunately, the capability of sanctions to harm the Iranian economy is in itself not enough to ensure that sanctions will deliver the desired outcome. Iranian leaders might calculate that the benefits of nuclear weapons outweigh the costs of sanctions. The challenge, then, is to inflict enough pain to force Iran's leaders to calculate that relief from sanctions (and the threat of military force and the prospect of additional inducements) is more desirable than continued pursuit of a nuclear weapon.

Sanctions do seem to have contributed to Iran's willingness to return to the negotiating table with the P5+1—the five permanent members of the UN Security Council (UNSC) and Germany—in April 2012; whether Iranian officials come to the table with the willingness to make needed concessions to get to a deal is a different matter. Thus far, there seems little evidence that economic pressure or increasing isolation wrought by sanctions are moving Iran's leaders to a more conciliatory position on their nuclear program. Admittedly, particularly with a regime as opaque as Iran's, it is difficult to assess how sanctions may be affecting the inner calculations of the government. As with all cases, the dilemma in assessing whether sanctions "are working" is that the government will claim such pressure has no bearing on its decision-making—until the moment it changes course.

Most experts on Iranian politics have concluded that the decision to proceed with or halt Iran's nuclear program—or at least the steps necessary to eventually realize one—lie squarely and perhaps solely with Supreme Leader Khamenei. How much economic duress would be needed for him to shift his thinking on an issue that has so defined his rule is unknown, but history suggests it would be extremely high. In all likelihood, sanctions and their impact would need to constitute some sort of threat to the survival of the regime before they could induce the sorts of concessions needed for Iran to be in compliance with UN and International Atomic Energy Agency (IAEA) demands.

Some configuration of sanctions could conceivably exact pain that exceeds this threshold, by depriving the government of the 50 to 70 percent of total revenues that come from oil sales. A near global, multilateral embargo on the purchase of Iranian oil would be a central component to such a sanctions regime; such an embargo might need to be accompanied by aggressive enforcement mechanisms, including a maritime blockade.

In practice, such a sanctions regime will be extremely difficult to construct. First, not all of Iran's customers would be willing to end their purchase of Iranian oil. For example, China has declared that it will implement only UN sanctions; China is Iran's largest single customer, buying about 20 percent of Iran's total oil exports, about $16 billion worth, in 2011. Second, Iran is well versed in smuggling and other ways of getting its oil to market; fully isolating it from global markets would be a huge challenge, even if the UN were enforcing a global ban. Third, a sanctions regime that prevented all Iranian oil from reaching international markets would place significant upward pressure on global oil prices, making many countries reluctant to institute such a ban at a time of global economic frailty. Fourth, a blockade to ensure the enforcement of the embargo would almost certainly be perceived as an act of war, adding to the reluctance of the international community to pursue such a policy path. Finally, such a draconian sanctions regime would meet with challenges on the humanitarian front. The suffering that resulted from comprehensive sanctions against Iraq from 1990 to 1995—and the complex and corrupt Oil for Food Program established in 1995 to mitigate its humanitarian effects—left most countries unwilling to revisit such policies.

The timeline under which sanctions must demonstrate results is presumably bounded by the limits of Israeli and U.S. patience on one end and Iran's ability to fashion a nuclear weapon on the other. As discussed elsewhere in this volume, in calendar terms an Iranian breakout timeline to produce weapons-grade material could be as little as a few months, once the Iranian leadership decides to do so. How long it would take Iran to weaponize that material is a much murkier subject. Given that the effects of sanctions generally cumulate over time, intensifying as a regime's mechanisms to cope run thin, expecting dramatic results from sanctions alone in this period of time is extremely ambitious.

One question almost never asked is how sanctions would perform if Iran did come to the negotiating table with serious intent to make a deal. In this circumstance, the desired role of sanctions would transform overnight from an instrument of pressure to a tool to supplement and reinforce the negotiations. Ideally, policymakers could promise and deliver sanctions relief as part of the overall effort to build confidence, induce gradual shifts in behavior, and reinforce contours of a new relationship. The current sanctions regime against Iran, however, would struggle—perhaps mightily—to adapt to this new raison d'être. The excessive layers of sanctions, the multiple U.S. and international actors that have imposed them, and their heavily congressionally inspired nature would make it hard for any policymaker to use sanctions relief in a nimble way in pursuit of a diplomatic deal. Deft use of sanctions (i.e., reducing them as an incentive and reward for desired behavior) would also be complicated by the reality that the United States would insist on keeping some sanctions in place to address Iran's support for terrorism, its opposition to Israel, and its human rights record.

UNINTENDED CONSEQUENCES OR BY-PRODUCTS OF A SANCTIONS-LED APPROACH

Although sanctions do not carry with them the weighty consequences of military action, they are not without their costs to the side imposing them. The costs borne by U.S. businesses forced to forgo commercial opportunities in Iran has commanded considerable attention, particularly because Chinese and other firms have willingly filled the gap. Other costs are more difficult to measure, but still warrant examination.

First, the current sanctions approach affects global energy security in a number of important ways. In threatening to frustrate the sale of

Iranian oil on the global market and in curtailing investment in Iran's energy sector over the long run, the sanctions contribute to actual and anticipated production disruptions. As mentioned, Iran is producing and selling less oil today than it has at any other time in the past decade; the International Energy Agency quotes industry sources saying that sanctions coming into force could mean that one million barrels of Iran's current exports come off the market in future months. Particularly in the current state of tight oil markets, with limited spare capacity in the system, both actual and anticipated production disruptions would force the price of oil higher. Simply the prospect of a military confrontation with Iran, which could jeopardize the 2.2 million b/d it contributes to the market or lead to the closure of the Strait of Hormuz for a period of time, has inflicted a significant geopolitical premium on the global price of oil. These price spikes can be mitigated by increased production by Saudi Arabia and other producers, although how seamlessly and how fully Riyadh can substitute its oil for Iranian oil or calm geopolitical jitters is uncertain.

A second unintended consequence is that the sanctions could motivate Iranian behavior, but not in the desired direction. For instance, the hardships imposed by sanctions could convince Tehran of what it has always been inclined to believe—that the real goal of the United States is to destroy the Islamic regime in Iran. Rather than inducing the government to abandon its pursuit of weapons, this conclusion could lead Tehran to expedite its nuclear program. Separately, the difficulties Iran is experiencing under the sanctions might also compel the Iranian government to undertake reforms and strategies it would otherwise avoid. Tehran has already made considerable progress in phasing out generous energy subsidies. It has also dedicated itself to building an indigenous refining capacity in order to reduce its vulnerability to outside pressure. As sanctions on International Monetary Fund (IMF) lending to Iran in the 1990s spurred Tehran to get its economic house in order, the sanctions of today might have the perverse effect of prompting Iran to rationalize its policies and thereby strengthen its economic foundations.

Finally, the sanctions on Iran are having geopolitical consequences beyond Iran, and in unexpected ways. U.S. and European policymakers have been sensitive to the risks associated with taking Iranian oil off global markets when little global spare capacity exists. For this reason, the sanctions are crafted more to lower the price Iran gets for its oil than to prevent the sale of Iranian oil. Countries willing to continue to buy Iranian oil can and are demanding discounts on what they pay for it. Effectively, this situation may amount to a stimulus program to the Chinese economy if China is able to buy large quantities of Iranian oil and pay below the market price for it. In another line of thinking, sanctions on Iran have inadvertently increased the stakes for political stability in other oil-producing countries. Stability in Baghdad and Riyadh—the two countries with the greatest potential to bring significant quantities of oil to market in the coming year—should take on a new importance, even as their facilities become more vulnerable to Iranian sabotage.

CONCLUSION

Sanctions against Iran today are a different animal than they have been. Thanks to a shared threat perception among the members of the international community, the focusing effect that the threat of Israeli force has provided, and new innovations in the financial realm, sanctions are inflicting serious harm on Iran's economy. The real challenge or achievement, however, is not the orchestration of this economic pain, but the translation of it into effective leverage in a successful negotiating strategy.

Prospects for a Negotiated Outcome

Richard A. Falkenrath

For more than thirty years, the United States and its international partners have struggled to find an effective diplomatic strategy toward Iran. Every administration since Carter has attempted, in one way or another and at one time or another, to establish a viable official dialogue with Iran to address the most pressing strategic issues of the day. And every administration has failed. The one partial and temporary exception to this pattern of diplomatic frustration was the constructive involvement of the government of Iran in crafting the initial post-Taliban political transition in Afghanistan in 2002 and 2003.[1]

The paramount strategic issue of 2012 for the United States and Israel is, clearly, the Iranian nuclear program. The issue has the look and feel of a major international security crisis in the making: occurring with the Arab Spring and the inconclusive Green Movement, the massive popular protests in Iran following the contested Iranian presidential elections of June 2009, fresh on everyone's mind, and against the backdrop of a U.S. presidential election. Intense, multifaceted economic sanctions are in place against Iran, hurting its already weak economy.[2] Four Iranian nuclear scientists have been assassinated on their morning commutes.[3] Extraordinarily sophisticated, covert, physical, and digital sabotage efforts are being directed against the Iranian nuclear program.[4] The possibility of military action against the Iranian nuclear complex is widely discussed in Washington, DC, in Jerusalem, and in other world capitals.

Diplomacy is of course an element of the international effort to defuse this brewing crisis. Whether to attempt to negotiate with Iran over its nuclear program is not in question. An active diplomatic effort around the Iranian nuclear program has been ongoing for several decades, with a wide variety of interlocutors, venues, objectives, and subtexts. The latest round of formal talks between Iran and the P5+1—the five permanent members of the United Nations Security Council (UNSC) and Germany—began in Istanbul on April 13, 2012.[5]

The resumption of P5+1 talks with Iran is itself something of a diplomatic achievement. In 2008, the P5+1 set an Iranian enrichment suspension as a precondition to formal negotiations. Similarly, the last round of such talks failed when Iran refused to engage in substantive discussions of its nuclear program unless its counterparts agreed to relax the extensive array of unilateral and military sanctions against Iran, and to acknowledge Iran's right to enrich uranium. Because the UNSC has for six years demanded that Iran "suspend all enrichment-related and reprocessing activities" (UN Security Council Resolution 1696), the P5+1 were in no position to meet Iran's precondition to talks. The April 2012 talks in Istanbul seem to indicate that Iran has now relaxed this precondition.

EVALUATING DIFFERENT NEGOTIATED OUTCOMES

Many countries and international organizations have a stake in the nuclear negotiations with Iran, even those that have no direct involvement in the P5+1 talks. Each has slightly different objectives as they approach the Iranian nuclear question. Some will be preeminently concerned with avoiding military conflict. Others will consider the commercial benefits that may accrue from different outcomes. Others may take a more traditional nonproliferation stance, and seek merely to return Iran to good standing with its Nuclear Nonproliferation Treaty (NPT) commitments. Some may be influenced by the impact of the Iranian issue on their domestic politics and their ability to retain their hold on political power via elections or other mechanisms.

At the beginning of the Istanbul round of talks in April 2012, three broad categories of possible negotiated outcomes were being discussed:

– the full suspension of all Iranian uranium enrichment and plutonium reprocessing operations, as called for in UN Security Council Resolution 1696

– an international fuel supply and retrieval arrangement for Iran, whereby Iran would forgo uranium enrichment in return for guaranteed fuel supplies from abroad[6]

– a commitment by Iran to limit its enrichment of uranium to 3 to 5 percent U-235, instead of the 20 percent it is currently producing

In addition, the P5+1 may also demand, as the United States has, that Iran halt construction at its deeply buried second enrichment facility at Fordow, and will certainly seek some sort of intrusive International Atomic Energy Agency (IAEA) inspections of Iran's nuclear complex and stores of nuclear materials.

With respect to each of these scenarios, there are serious questions about whether the P5+1 is even united enough to propose any of them specifically; what, if any, concessions the P5+1 would offer Iran as an inducement; and whether Iran would respond positively or even constructively. Because these matters are being played out in real time as this volume goes to press, they are not examined here.

It is, however, possible to evaluate the expected nonproliferation benefits of each of these outcomes, using the metric described in Ray Takeyh's introduction: "The appropriate metric for judging nonproliferation and disarmament agreements is thus not whether they eliminate a country's option of acquiring nuclear weapons, which is impossible, but instead the time they reliably extend a country's weaponization timetable."

In the first scenario of a possible diplomatic outcome of the P5+1 talks with Iran, a full suspension of all known Iranian uranium enrichment and plutonium reprocessing would reliably extend the country's weaponization timetable for as long as the suspension was in effect, unless Iran had a separate enrichment capability unknown to the international community.[7] The reason is that to build a basic nuclear weapon, Iran requires multiple kilograms of highly enriched uranium (HEU, approximately 90 percent U-235) or plutonium, both of which Iran currently lacks. During the suspension, Iran could work on the wide range of other technical tasks associated with building and deploying militarily useful nuclear weapons, which would over time have the effect of shortening Iran's timetable for weapons assembly. And Iran could use the respite to "immunize" itself from the threat of preventive Israeli or American military action by constructing larger underground facilities (like Fordow) that are truly impervious to conventional military attack, thus giving itself a better option to "break out" and construct nuclear weapons at some future date. But the net effect would probably be a positive one from a nonproliferation standpoint—that is, a full suspension of Iranian enrichment and reprocessing would extend the country's weaponization timetable for at least the first few years of the suspension (unless, of course, Iran cheated in some manner).

In the second scenario, a comprehensive international fuel supply and retrieval arrangement for Iran, in which it forgoes domestic uranium enrichment in return for guaranteed fuel supplies from abroad, could in principle have nonproliferation effects identical to a full suspension of all known Iranian uranium enrichment and plutonium reprocessing. For as long as the international fuel supply and retrieval arrangement were in place alongside a full enrichment and reprocessing suspension, Iran's weaponization timetable would extend until Iran managed to shorten it again by making progress on the other technical aspects of nuclear weapons construction, by immunizing itself from future preventative military threats, or by cheating.

The third scenario, in which Iran commits to limit its enrichment of uranium to 3 to 5 percent U-235, instead of the 20 percent it is currently producing, would have no reliable impact on its weaponization timetable except in the immediate term—that is, the next year or two. As noted, Iran cannot construct nuclear weapons until it has multiple kilograms of HEU or separated plutonium. Uranium enrichment is a cumulative process, in which, given a particular enrichment infrastructure, precisely calculable amounts of time and energy are required to raise the enrichment level of a given quantity of uranium to a given enrichment level. In the nuclear fuel industry, the measurement of enrichment work is standardized and expressed in terms of separative work units (SWU). A cap on the level to which Iran can enrich is irrelevant if there is no cap on the total amount of SWU it can expend in its enrichment operations. If Iran decides it wants 90 percent enriched HEU, it can feed either a large quantity of 3 percent enriched uranium into its cascades or a smaller quantity of 20 percent enriched; in both cases, it will achieve its desired quantity of 90 percent enriched HEU more quickly and with less energy than if it used natural uranium as feedstock; the difference has mainly to do with the amount of SWU in the feedstock, not its enrichment level. To appreciate this technical point, consider the analogy of a man climbing a staircase who promises not to take three steps at a time; why would one think he wouldn't eventually reach the top of the staircase if he can still take one step at a time?

Of course, any of these outcomes, if accepted by Iran, would likely have the effect of temporarily defusing the immediate geopolitical crisis. The price of oil would fall. The international community could turn its attention to other matters.

But whether the nonproliferation benefits of the agreement are more than illusory will depend on the details of the agreement and on Iran's strategic choices about what sort of nuclear capability it wants at what time in the future. As has been made abundantly clear from the North Korean experience, a country's nuclear weaponization timetable is not solely a function of the amount of fissile material it produces at IAEA-inspected facilities. A country can halt fissile material production at an IAEA-inspected facility but continue to produce in secret elsewhere, as North Korea did; it can separately pursue research and development along a wide range of different technical avenues important to the deployment of a viable nuclear weapon, such as weapons and delivery vehicle design, which have the effect of shortening and reducing the risk of a country's weaponization timetable; and it can construct better protected fissile material and nuclear weapons production facilities, thus immunizing itself from future preventive military threats.

CONCLUSION

At present, based on the historical record, the prospect that the current Iranian government, with its nationalist ideology and domestic instability, will consent to any significant, verifiable curtailment of its program to give itself the option of constructing nuclear weapons is effectively zero. This is not to say that the P5+1 should not engage in nuclear diplomacy with Iran, only that they should not accept a deal that is no more than temporarily palliative. Nuclear negotiations with Iran today cannot solve the Iranian nuclear problem; instead, the immediate aims of talks should be modest, technical, and perceptual. The real value of these talks is likely to play out over the longer term by creating conditions in which the international community is increasingly united and resolute with respect to Iran, and other Iranian leaders may have the latitude and the incentive to accept constraints that effectively lengthen the Iranian weaponization timetable.

It is not clear how such a negotiated arrangement would affect domestic Iranian politics. On the one hand, Iranian nationalists and populists may decry any agreement as a subornation of Iranian sovereignty; on the other, ordinary Iranian citizens may appreciate a reduction in economic sanctions and international ostracization. But if one thing is predictable, it is that the Iranian regime is unlikely to consent to any such agreement if it believes the agreement will harm the regime's legitimacy and political standing. Therefore, at least in the mind of the Iranian leaders, a nuclear agreement worth signing is an agreement that will help, not hurt, the regime's hold on political power in Iran.

So what, then, should be the purpose of nuclear negotiations with Iran? An alternative to the traditional nonproliferation approach would be to treat the negotiations with Iran not as a real opportunity to extend the Iranian nuclear weaponization timetable, which President Mahmoud Ahmadinejad and the clerical regime give no reason to believe is a realistic scenario, but instead as an opportunity for high-level global signaling toward two basic audiences and with a post-Ahmadinejad regime in mind. The first audience would be the Iranian people and Ahmadinejad's various political rivals, if not the Iranian theocracy. The second audience would be the other international actors, most important the two most recalcitrant permanent members of the Security Council—Russia and China—along with the major states of Europe.

For both audiences, the purpose of the negotiations would be the same: to shift the perceptual balance against Ahmadinejad and all other populist, nationalist Iranian leaders by openly presenting Iran with a nuclear restraint framework—possibly along the lines of the P5+1 comprehensive proposal of June 2008—so reasonable, so generous, and so respectful of Iranian sensibilities that Iran's turning it down would only vivify the regime's unreasonableness. Iran should be dared to say yes. In the unlikely event that it does, negotiation of the detailed implementation agreement may drag on for months, possibly until the Iranian presidential elections in June 2013. In the meantime, economic sanctions and political pressure against Iran would continue to mount, but with the onus of responsibility shifted to the greatest extent possible to the deceitful and difficult leadership in Tehran. The risk of military action would continue to loom, and the failure of another round of nuclear talks with Iran could help shape the international environment that makes various more aggressive options—a blockade, or even preventive airstrikes—less diplomatically catastrophic.

There is of course no guarantee that Ahmadinejad or the clerics behind him will recede from political ascendency anytime soon, or that his successors will be any more inclined to extend the Iranian nuclear weaponization timetable, or that the ayatollahs who currently hold ultimate political power in the Islamic Republic will permit any elected, civilian government to compromise Iran's nuclear agenda. But, as shown by the Arab Spring and, two decades earlier, the collapse of the Soviet Union, political tides can and sometimes do turn swiftly against repressive governments. Moreover, governments do from time to time decide to relinquish incipient nuclear weapons programs or even nuclear arsenals: consider Taiwan, Argentina, Brazil, South Africa, South Korea, Ukraine, Belarus, Kazakhstan, and Libya.[8] For this reason, a diplomatic strategy geared principally at communicating reasonableness, benign intent, and resolve to a future cadre of Iranian leaders has a certain appeal when more tangible, near-term diplomatic achievements seem unattainable or to have only illusory benefits.

Assessing Israel's Military Option

Matthew Kroenig

When Prime Minister Benjamin Netanyahu of Israel visited Washington, DC, in March 2012, he gave President Barack Obama a copy of the Book of Esther, a gift that an aide described as "background reading on Iran."[1] The message was not subtle. The Book of Esther tells the story of an ancient Persian plot to annihilate the Jewish people.

For years, Israeli officials have warned that a nuclear-armed Iran would pose an existential threat to the state of Israel. Although it is unlikely that Iran would intentionally launch a suicidal nuclear war, a future crisis between a nuclear-armed Iran and Israel could spiral out of control and into catastrophe. Given Israel's small size and lack of strategic depth, it would be particularly vulnerable to any nuclear attack.

For Israel, therefore, the stakes could not be higher. And given Israel's successful preventive strikes on nuclear reactors in Iraq in 1981 and Syria in 2007, it is no surprise that Israeli officials are seriously contemplating an attack on Iran's nuclear facilities.[2] But will Israel actually conduct such a strike? Would it be successful? And what are the likely consequences for international peace and security and for U.S. interests?

WHAT WOULD MAKE ISRAEL GO?

Israel's decision to conduct a strike on Iran's nuclear facilities would almost certainly be driven by a desire to move before its window of opportunity for effective military action against Iran's nuclear program closes.[3] As will be discussed, Israel has a limited ability to inflict serious damage on Iran's underground uranium facilities at Natanz and especially at Qom.[4] As Iran moves more of its sensitive nuclear work into the well-protected facility at Qom, Israel's leaders fear that Iran might enter a "zone of immunity," a point at which a significant portion of Iran's nuclear program would survive an Israeli attack.[5] Unlike the United States, which has a greater ability to destroy buried and hardened targets, Israel cannot afford to wait to strike until Iran makes a final dash to construct nuclear weapons.[6] Given Iran's stated plans for expanding its nuclear work at Qom over the coming months, this point of no return could come by the end of 2012.[7]

Israel's window of opportunity could continue to remain open if Iran halted its nuclear work at Qom as part of a diplomatic agreement with the West. As Richard Falkenrath discusses elsewhere in this volume, however, such a deal is unlikely for several reasons.

Israel could also be restrained from attacking if its leaders were convinced that Washington would strike if necessary to prevent Iran from acquiring nuclear weapons.[8] Indeed, Israel would prefer that the United States, with its superior capabilities, take the lead in destroying Iran's nuclear plants.[9] But it is unlikely that the U.S. president would make a final decision on this issue until forced to do so. And, for Israel, it will be difficult to outsource responsibility for national security to another country, even if that country is the United States.

At the other extreme, Israel could become emboldened to strike if it received an explicit green light and pledges of support from Washington, but this scenario seems unlikely. The George W. Bush and Obama administrations have both discouraged an Israeli attack, and there is little reason to believe that this position will change in the foreseeable future.[10]

WHAT WOULD AN ISRAELI OPERATION LOOK LIKE?

As many outside analysts have written, an Israeli strike on Iran's nuclear facilities would be a difficult operation.[11] Israel's fleet of American F-15 and F-16 fighters would have to fly over two thousand kilometers across foreign territory (most likely due east over Jordan and Iraq, although there are other possible routes), conduct aerial refueling to extend the aircrafts' ranges, contend with the Iranian air defenses, strike their intended targets, and race back to defend against possible counterattack from Iran and its proxies.[12]

Unlike the United States, which would have the option of targeting Iranian air defenses, Iran's military retaliatory capabilities, and a wide range of facilities involved in the nuclear program, Israel would be constrained to attacking a few of Iran's most important nuclear facilities. The target set would most likely include the uranium conversion facility at Esfahan, the plutonium-producing reactor under construction at Arak, the uranium enrichment facilities at Natanz and Qom, and possibly the light-water reactors at Bushehr.[13]

The facilities at Esfahan, Arak, and Bushehr are aboveground and would be vulnerable to Israeli air strikes. The uranium enrichment facility at Natanz, however, is buried under seventy-five feet of earth and several meters of reinforced concrete.[14] And the Fordow facility outside Qom is built into the side of a mountain and is thus covered by 295 feet of rock.[15] To strike these facilities, Israel could use its arsenal of American-provided bunker-busting bombs, but these munitions are capable of penetrating only twenty feet of concrete or one hundred feet of earth.[16] They would be unable, therefore, to penetrate the Natanz and Fordow facilities in a single shot. Israel might be able, however, to destroy Natanz by tunneling—putting bunker busters in the crater created by previous strikes. As former commander of the Israel Air Force General Eitan Ben-Elyahu said, "Even if one bomb would not suffice to penetrate, we could guide other bombs directly to the hole created by the previous ones and eventually destroy any target."[17] Even using this technique, it is unlikely that Israel could damage Qom. Israel could, however, render both buried facilities unusable for at least several months by destroying their entrances, air shafts, and power and water systems.[18] In short, an Israeli strike would almost certainly destroy some of Iran's most critical nuclear facilities and significantly damage others.

WHAT ARE THE LIKELY CONSEQUENCES?

The principal benefit of an Israeli strike is that it would delay Iran's progress toward a nuclear bomb. U.S. officials have estimated publicly that this delay could be two to three years.[19] These estimates, however, appear to assume that Iran immediately decides to reconstitute its program as quickly as possible and does not encounter substantial subsequent difficulties. If Iran decided to let the dust settle before reconstituting, or encounters other problems along the way, these timelines would be longer. And it is always possible that the delay creates space for other events to transpire, such as an Iranian decision to abandon the program, further diplomacy with the international community, an indigenous regime change, or future military conflict, any of which could prevent Iran from acquiring nuclear weapons indefinitely.

Some argue that a strike could actually put Iran closer to a weapon by removing any remaining doubt among Iran's leaders about whether to weaponize; giving them an excuse to end negotiations, kick out international inspectors, drive the program further underground, and withdraw from the Nuclear Nonproliferation Treaty (NPT); weakening the international consensus against Iran's nuclear program; and encouraging Tehran to move with all haste toward a bomb.

Iran's nuclear program is already advancing rapidly, however, and is clearly aimed at developing a nuclear weapons capability. Leaving the NPT or throwing out inspectors would certainly limit U.S. knowledge of future Iranian nuclear activity and complicate any subsequent decisions to strike again, but Iran could, regardless, choose to take the same actions to build a bomb. The development of a redundant and better-protected program would certainly make subsequent strikes more difficult, but it would also be resource intensive and time consuming. In short, a strike would likely make subsequent strikes harder and complicate future efforts at diplomacy, but there is little doubt that it would, at a minimum, set back Iran's nuclear progress.

An Israeli strike would also have more serious consequences, the most obvious of which is Iranian military retaliation. Iran does not maintain a strong conventional military and has focused on developing asymmetric military options, including cultivating ties to terrorist and proxy groups, developing ballistic missiles of varying ranges, and building irregular naval forces that could cause mayhem in the Persian Gulf.[20] In the aftermath of an Israeli attack, Iran might well lash out in response and unleash its riskiest retaliatory options.

At least as likely, however, is that Iran would try to carefully navigate its strategic dilemma. On the one hand, it would want to strike back hard enough to save face domestically and reestablish deterrence internationally. On the other, it would want to avoid provoking a major war that might lead to the destruction of the regime. An additional constraint on Iranian retaliation would be Iran's desire to maintain military forces to deter future conflict. If Iran launched its entire arsenal of ballistic missiles or picked a fight that resulted in the destruction of the Iranian navy, for example, it would leave itself defenseless. In short, there is reason to believe that Iran's leaders might aim for some kind of calibrated response. It is always possible, however, that Iran could miscalculate and provoke a larger conflict than it intended.

Tehran's most likely initial response from an Israeli strike, therefore, could be to encourage rocket fire from Hamas and Hezbollah into Israel, launch several salvos of Shahab-3 missiles into Israel, and harass, and possibly attack, commercial and naval ships in the Persian Gulf. Iran might choose to aim its ballistic missiles at Israeli population centers, but it might also choose to target only Israeli military and nuclear facilities, such as Israel's nuclear reactor at Dimona. Indeed, this might be what Iran's supreme leader had in mind when he recently promised to respond to any attack "at the same level" of the aggressors.[21]

Of course, the full range of military consequences would depend in large part on U.S. and Israeli responses. The conflict could spread if Israel decided to invade Gaza or southern Lebanon in response to Hamas or Hezbollah rocket fire, or if Jerusalem decided to strike back directly against Iran. U.S. intervention could also widen the conflict. If Iran were to limit itself to a token retaliation against Israeli targets only, it is likely that the United States would stay out of the conflict and seek to quickly de-escalate the crisis. If, however, Iran retaliated directly against U.S. forces, ships, or bases, or was behind massive and more lethal attacks against Israel, it is likely that the United States would enter the conflict, resulting in the consequences described in Robert D. Blackwill's chapter in this volume.

An Israeli attack would also lead to a spike in oil prices, hampering economic growth at a fragile time for the global economy. A strike would immediately lead to price increases as speculators bid up the price of oil, but the size and duration of any price increase would depend largely on the size and duration of any supply disruptions. More devastating would be an Iranian attempt to close the Strait of Hormuz, which would compel the United States to use military force to reopen it, possibly preventing any oil from passing through the strait for several weeks. This scenario could cause the price of a barrel of oil to increase by $200 for the duration of the conflict.

An attack on Iran could also produce a rally-around-the-flag effect, temporarily strengthening the ruling regime. This effect could dissipate with time, however, and the strike could even weaken the regime by creating an opportunity for opposition groups to criticize the government for bringing a crisis to the country and for squandering the popular nuclear program.

Other second- and third-order consequences to a strike are pos-sible. An Israeli strike could harm the reputation of the United States in the Muslim and Arab worlds and around the globe because many would assume American complicity, even if the attack were conducted against the White House's wishes. It could also affect the strength of the global nonproliferation regime. For example, it might encourage other states to acquire nuclear weapons to avoid attack. Conversely, it might strengthen nonproliferation by convincing would-be proliferators that violating the NPT carries certain consequences.

None of these consequences is immutable, however. Indeed, the United States could do much to mitigate the negative fallout. Wash-ington could seek to encourage a restrained Iranian military response by issuing a deterrent threat in the aftermath of an attack. It could also announce that it was not a participant in the strike, but that, if Iran responds militarily, the United States would be forced to enter the con-flict, with potentially devastating consequences for Iran. This threat, along with private reassurances to Jerusalem, could also prevent Israel from enlarging the conflict. The United States could also seek to hold down oil prices by encouraging increased Saudi production and open-ing the Strategic Petroleum Reserve, or to use an Israeli strike as an opportunity to weaken the current Iranian government in a carefully designed public diplomacy campaign.

In conclusion, this comprehensive assessment of Israel's military option for U.S. interests suggests a few genuine benefits and many potential costs. Whether this option is superior to the alternatives, however, will depend largely on the true values of many unpredictable parameters. It is possible that an Israeli strike might destroy many of Iran's most important nuclear facilities, that Iran responds with only token retaliation, and that the United States is able to work diplomati-cally to quickly defuse the crisis. If the U.S. government could know this to be the case, an Israeli strike would have to rank, from Washing-ton's perspective, as a relatively attractive outcome. It is also possible, however, that an Israeli strike does minimal damage to Iran's nuclear program yet unleashes the full range of downside consequences. It is for fear of this latter scenario that one must also carefully consider the advantages and disadvantages of the other options outlined elsewhere in this volume.

A U.S. Attack on Iran

Robert D. Blackwill

Considering the profound question of whether the United States should preventively attack Iran to slow its nuclear weapons program, those who oppose such U.S. military action appear to almost never seriously ask George Marshall's persistent policy question, "Why might I be wrong?" These pundits tend to dismiss the acutely troubling regional and global implications of Iran's acquisition of nuclear weapons, including markedly strengthening Iran's power projection and hegemonic ambitions, and the dangers of nuclear proliferation in the Middle East with the chance of a nuclear war in that exceptionally unstable region. They discount the possibility that under certain extreme conditions Iran might transfer nuclear weapons technology to other nations or terrorist groups. They ignore the potentially damaging effect on American power, influence, and credibility in the region of U.S. acquiescence to Iran's nuclear weapons capability after successive administrations have said for many years that it was "unacceptable."

At the same time, emotion and high-blown rhetoric often seem to rule the day for proponents of an American-initiated clash with Iran, rather than cold-calculated estimates of the potential costs and benefits. After all, this would be the fourth U.S. attack on a Muslim nation in a little over a decade, and the fifth if U.S. military forces engage Syria in the foreseeable future. With this record, perhaps it is unsurprising that a popular view in the Islamic world is that the United States is inherently anti-Muslim, a sentiment that complicates American calculations regarding an attack on Iran. Consistent with the times, such intensely held but one-sided advocacy unfortunately often dominates public discourse on this complicated subject.

In examining the inherent intricacies of U.S. military action against Iran, the following questions are central:

– What would precipitate a U.S. attack on Iran?

– What would be the objectives of such American military operations?

- What would be the target set?
- How long would the attack last?
- What would be the potential Iranian reactions to the U.S. attack, and over what timeline?
- What would be the intensity, duration, and consequences of the regional and international reaction to such an attack?
- How would the United States cope with the Iranian and international reaction?

WHAT WOULD PRECIPITATE A U.S. ATTACK ON IRAN?

For an American president to make the historic decision to attack Iran, the following conditions presumably should have been met. First, the U.S. administration would have determined that an Iranian nuclear weapons capability would represent an abiding threat to U.S. vital national interests. Today, this is the overwhelming view of American policymakers, politicians, and the public.

Second, the administration would have concluded that the Iranian leadership had decided to acquire an actual or latent nuclear arsenal, that it had crossed this red line. The difficulty here is that U.S. intelligence directed against this particularly hard target may well not uncover in time such an operational decision by the small Iranian leadership circle that would make such a determination, and that subsequent weaponization (if it is not already occurring) could be secretly conducted without American discovery. As David Sanger at the *New York Times* has pointed out, the American intelligence community "missed the timing of the first Soviet nuclear test in 1949, to President Harry S. Truman's outrage. They also got the timing wrong on China in the 1960s, India in the '70s and Pakistan in the '80s," though in all those cases no International Atomic Energy Agency (IAEA) inspectors were on the ground, as they have been in Iran.[1]

Third, neither international sanctions nor negotiations would have promised an acceptable solution to this problem in an acceptable time frame. Again, this will be critically a matter of presidential judgment, because Iran will never admit that biting sanctions would coerce it to suspend its nuclear weapon activities until, if, and when it decides to do so. And as Henry Kissinger points out in another context, the bureaucratic temptation will be strong to give sanctions and diplomacy one more day/week/month/year to succeed if the alternative is going to war. Fourth, cyber and other covert means would not have satisfactorily delayed the Iranian nuclear programs. And fifth, to be worth it, the benefits of such an attack would have been judged by the president to outweigh the negative regional and global consequences.

WHAT WOULD BE THE OBJECTIVES
OF SUCH AMERICAN MILITARY OPERATIONS?

The purpose of a preventive U.S. attack on Iran would be to use air and sea power to set back for many years its nuclear weapons programs and ideally to lead the Iranian leadership to abandon those dangerous and destabilizing nuclear activities. (The chances of an American ground invasion and occupation of Iran seem so remote as to not justify further examination here.) Unlike the hypothetical Israeli attack discussed in the previous chapter, there is no doubt that the unmatched U.S. military, if it mounted concerted combat operations against Iran, could substantially delay an Iranian effort to acquire nuclear weapons capabilities. However, experts disagree on how long a U.S. attack would interrupt and postpone Iran's nuclear weapons activities. Advocates of a decisive U.S. military operation assert that it would take years for Tehran to rebuild its nuclear infrastructure, whereas critics argue that it would take much less time, perhaps twenty-four or fewer months. This is obviously an important variable in a presidential decision on whether to launch a U.S. attack on Iran.

WHAT WOULD BE THE TARGET SET?

There is no attempt here to duplicate the work of the attack planners for the Joint Chiefs of Staff at the Pentagon. Nevertheless, some generalizations can be drawn from the public record. Given the potential negative consequences of an American attack on Iran, as well as the multiplicity of targets associated with the Iranian nuclear program, it seems unlikely that the president would approve a small raid.

Rather, it appears probable that dozens of the estimated seventy or so Iranian nuclear facilities, associated air defenses, and perhaps ballistic missile installations would be hit by a combination of combat fighter aircraft, B-1 and B-2 bombers, and air-and-sea-launched cruise missiles. The most important targets would be the hardened and buried uranium enrichment facility at Natanz and the Fordow uranium enrichment facility in a mountain near Qom; the plutonium-producing reactor under construction at Arak; the uranium conversion facility at Esfahan; possibly the nuclear reactors at Bushehr; and whatever sites in which known or suspected weaponization activities might occur. If all these facilities were successfully destroyed or heavily damaged, the Iranian nuclear effort might be set back by five or more years, a substantial accomplishment.

Nevertheless, a further complication arises in the possibility that U.S. intelligence may not have uncovered duplicative Iranian nuclear installations, which could prejudice the overall success of the air assault. A lengthier and more comprehensive American attack, which had regime change as a crucial objective, seems less likely and would in addition target the Revolutionary Guard Corps, intelligence agencies, political leadership, conventional forces, and oil and gas infrastructure.

HOW LONG WOULD THE ATTACK LAST?

In view of the expected widespread international condemnation of such an attack, especially within the Arab and broader Muslim world, ideally it would be brief, perhaps only a few hours. However, the United States might not be able to achieve its primary military goals in such a short time. Instead, to meet operational objectives U.S. forces might have to return to the targets multiple times over many days in hundreds or thousands of sorties. Indeed, arguably the worst outcome of an American attack on Iran would be to do the job halfway and ineffectively, delaying Iranian progress only a year or two, thus generating the negative consequences of such U.S. military operations (Iranian reactions and international censure) without sufficiently slowing Iranian nuclear programs.

But if an extended U.S. air assault on Iran lasting several days or longer were required, one can easily imagine both severe global pressure—including in the UN Security Council—for the United States to cease and desist as well as pervasive violence against U.S. government and business facilities throughout the Middle East, violence that most regimes in the region would be unable or unwilling to stop. Finally, a prolonged U.S. air campaign might well make Iranian escalation more likely. The trade-offs here are therefore thorny. One might recall the views of Winston Churchill: "Let us learn our lessons.... Never believe any war will be smooth and easy or that anyone who embarks on that strange voyage can measure the tides and hurricanes he will encounter. The statesman who yields to war fever must realize that once the signal is given, he is no longer the master of policy but the slave of unforeseeable and uncontrollable events . . . incompetent or arrogant commanders, untrustworthy allies, hostile neutrals, malignant fortune, ugly surprise, awful miscalculations."[2]

WHAT WOULD BE THE POTENTIAL IRANIAN REACTIONS TO THE U.S. ATTACK, AND OVER WHAT TIMELINE?

This question is perhaps the most perplexing related to this subject. Because U.S. intelligence has few insights into the internal decision-making processes of the Iranian government, it is exceedingly difficult to put odds on the likely reactions of Tehran to an American attack, not least because we do not have a firm understanding of the regime's perceptions of its national interests. To simplify that problem, it is tempting to apply a rational actor model to Tehran's tactical and strategic choices. In a press interview in February 2012, the chairman of the Joint Chiefs of Staff described Iran as a "rational actor" whose leaders presumably are overwhelmingly concerned with preserving their regime and their power. And as Tom Schelling has emphasized, "You can sit in your armchair and try to predict how people will behave by asking how you would behave if you had your wits around you."[3] But more or less using that technique, the United States has continually been surprised by the actions of other governments: Hitler in the 1930s, Pearl Harbor, the Bay of Pigs, Soviet erection of the Berlin Wall, the Tet Offensive, the fall of the Shah, Saddam Hussein's invasion of Kuwait, the collapse of the Soviet Union, the Taliban revival in Afghanistan, the length of the recent war in Libya, and so forth.

In the context of a U.S. strike, Iran's leadership would in the first instance face a decisive and far-reaching choice that the United States would presumably attempt to shape. Would Tehran respond in a fashion that sought to avoid escalation of the conflict and maximize its perception in world opinion as the innocent and aggrieved victim of

American anti-Islamic aggression, or would it act in ways that made a comprehensive and extended U.S. military operation against Iran more likely? Obviously the United States would like to avoid a long war and thus encourage a restrained Iranian reaction, but could Washington put together a target set and attack plan large enough to slow the Iranian nuclear program for many years, yet modest enough to minimize the likelihood of major Iranian escalation? As discussed in other chapters, it is also unclear whether Iranian citizens would solidify behind the regime in such circumstances and how much the dimensions of a U.S. attack might affect Iranian public opinion.

Supreme Leader Ayatollah Ali Khamenei, speaking on state television on March 20, 2012, said that all of Iran's conventional firepower was ready to respond to any attack. "But against an attack by enemies—to defend ourselves either against the U.S. or Zionist regime—we will attack them on the same level that they attack us." Given Washington's weak predictive record and the fog of war in conditions of incomplete information, it seems wise for contingency purposes to take Khamenei at his word and then some, to be prepared as much as possible before mounting an attack for any and all of Iran's potential escalatory actions.

An Iranian escalatory ladder from bottom to top, incorporating asymmetric warfare, might look something like the following, including when applied to the contingencies that the United States could be drawn into a war with Iran begun by an attack by Israel or by a U.S. naval blockade:

– End all negotiations with the West on its nuclear programs.

– Begin immediately to accelerate, rebuild, disperse, and hide its nuclear facilities with even more determination to acquire nuclear weapons as a deterrent to future U.S. attacks (to avoid Saddam Hussein's and Qaddafi's fate), leaving the Nuclear Nonproliferation Treaty (NPT) and expelling IAEA inspectors.

– Persuade or coerce Muslim countries to positively restructure their relations with Iran, taking advantage of anti-American public opinion in the context of the Arab Awakening, and to sever diplomatic relations with the United States.

– Promote an oil boycott against the United States and its allies that could undermine the world economy.

– Encourage domestic unrest in Arab countries friendly to the United States.

– Prompt massive Hezbollah and Hamas missile barrages against Israel.

– Attack Israel with Shahab ballistic missiles, attempting to draw Israel into the war.

– Conduct clandestine violence against American facilities and citizens throughout the Muslim world and beyond.

– Increase material support for Taliban operations against U.S. forces in Afghanistan and radical Shia terrorism against U.S. facilities and personnel in Iraq.

– Target energy production facilities in the region.

– Attack U.S. warships in and mine the Persian Gulf, or attempt to close the Strait of Hormuz, through which 20 percent of world oil trade passes, thus producing a sharp spike in global oil prices.

– Use ballistic missiles to attack U.S. military installations in the Gulf.

– Conduct terrorist operations, including through Hezbollah agents in the United States and Latin America, against the American homeland, possibly using chemical and even biological weapons.

WHAT WOULD BE THE INTENSITY, DURATION, AND CONSEQUENCES OF THE REGIONAL AND INTERNATIONAL REACTION TO SUCH AN ATTACK?

It would be the task of American diplomacy in the weeks and months leading up to the war to try to convince the world that, as Cicero put it, "Let war be so carried on that no other object may seem to be sought but the acquisition of peace." But given the current negative positions of most governments on the matter, it seems plausible that a U.S. preventive attack on Iran would meet with widespread international denunciation at the outset, including from some nations that would privately applaud American success in substantially slowing the Iranian nuclear program. Washington could perhaps minimize such an international reaction to some degree were it to have previously demonstrated that it had attempted to reach a fair and lasting negotiated settlement with Iran, which Tehran had rejected, and were it to have stressed that the attack had the limited objective of destroying the Iranian nuclear weapons complex. The apparent success or failure of a U.S. attack, including the avoidance of civilian casualties, would also have some influence on the regional and global reaction. As indicated earlier, one could expect an immediate UN Security Council (UNSC) resolution condemning the U.S. action for which most of the UNSC, perhaps including the United States' closest allies, would vote. Russia and China would be particularly adamant. A UN General Assembly vote would have a similar result. Moreover, the effect of a U.S. attack against Iran in the currently wobbly Arab Middle East could be destabilizing.

But if the attack were relatively brief and American diplomacy had cleared the way, if its results were clearly positive and if Iran did not significantly escalate the conflict, this international furor might be short lived. Many countries taking their own national interests into account would have considerable incentive to maintain good relations with Washington. But should the war drag on, and especially if it sent energy prices through the roof and disrupted the already troubled global economy, the crescendo of criticism against the United States could be expected to grow and affect the U.S. government's capacity to do business with nations around the world.

HOW WOULD THE UNITED STATES COPE WITH THE IRANIAN AND INTERNATIONAL REACTION?

Even though the United States is presently engaged in the longest period of war in its history, current polling suggests that, if adequately prepared, the American people would support a U.S.-initiated war to attempt to stop Iran from acquiring nuclear weapons. In a February 2012 Pew Research Center poll, 58 percent of those surveyed said the United States should use military force, if necessary, to prevent Iran from developing nuclear weapons. Only 30 percent said no. How long that public backing would last, including for follow-up attacks on Iran if it sought to rebuild its nuclear infrastructure, is difficult to predict and would be crucially affected by the intensity and duration of the conflict and by whether it directly affected the lives of ordinary Americans through reprisal attacks in the United States, weakening of the American economy, and higher gasoline prices.

With that as context, this advice from the father of strategy, Sun Tsu, in his book *The Art of War* may be pertinent: "He who wishes to fight must first count the cost. When you engage in actual fighting, if victory is long in coming, then men's weapons will grow dull and their ardor will be dampened. If you lay siege to a town, you will exhaust your strength. Again, if the campaign is protracted, the resources of the State will not be equal to the strain. Now, when your weapons are dulled, your ardor dampened, your strength exhausted and your treasure spent, other chieftains will spring up to take advantage of your extremity. Then no man, however wise, will be able to avert the consequences that must ensue." But despite this ancient perspective, if U.S. vital national interests are severely threatened by Iranian acquisition of latent or actual nuclear weapons capability, the American president should not be paralyzed by either the complexities or the possible length of a conflict with Iran.

Regime Change

Elliott Abrams

Years of American efforts to change the behavior of the Islamic Republic of Iran have met with almost uniform failure. For the United States, Iran's nuclear weapons program, its intervention in Iraq and Afghanistan, its support of terrorism, its threats against Israel, and its internal repression are all objectionable, and all have proved largely impervious to U.S. pressure. Even now, with remarkably harsh international sanctions in place and visibly harming Iran's economy, the regime's policies appear unaffected.

It is therefore unsurprising that a different approach has been suggested: regime change. If the Islamic Republic is not reformable, and is immovable on critical issues of concern to the United States, perhaps the best policy is to seek its demise. That would resolve most of the United States' differences with Iran, or so it is argued. By regime change is meant the fall of the Islamic Republic and its replacement with a different system, presumably far more democratic, not theocratic, and without the current regime's deep hostility to the United States.

Perhaps the first question to ask is whether a different regime in Tehran would indeed be likely to resolve America's relationship with Iran. Then, one can look at what the United States might do to produce regime change, whether such actions have a chance of succeeding, what their costs might be, and what alternatives exist.

Iran and the United States do not have a history of perennial rivalry and hostility. The usual assessment of Iranian popular opinion toward the United States is positive despite three decades of hostile official propaganda. It is not Iran's history or culture but the Islamic Republic that has cast the United States as the "Great Satan." A different regime in Tehran seems likely to pull back from the (literal) demonization of the United States and Israel, be far less repressive at home, and end support for terrorism.

Would it abandon its nuclear program? Polls suggest that the Iranian public wants nuclear energy but not nuclear weapons.[1] It is reasonable to expect that a new, democratic regime in Iran would follow the path of others, such as South Africa and Brazil, developing nuclear energy but ending the military aspects of the program. Furthermore, the strength of objection to any nation's possession of nuclear weapons depends largely on the assessment of its government and how responsibly its leaders act. Even a nuclear weapons program by a new regime in Tehran would be far less dangerous than the current situation, for even if the United States and Iran had opposing views on a number of issues, Iran would not be so threatening to its Gulf neighbors, the United States, and Israel.

Why, then, does the United States not have a policy of regime change, for example, seeking to create political instability and economic turmoil, arming rebels against Tehran, and urging Iranians to rise up to overthrow their rulers?

First, if decision-makers assume that regime survival is the Iranian regime's central goal, such a policy might elicit even worse conduct than they now see. The Islamic Republic does support terrorism and has created instability in Iraq and Afghanistan, but it has a capacity for far more disturbing conduct: assassinating heads of state, creating mass casualties, and providing far more deadly weaponry to terrorist groups, for example. It could seek actively to destabilize neighboring states, especially those with large Shia populations. If the rulers in Tehran conclude that the United States is trying to overthrow them, there could be a heavy price to pay unless and until Washington succeeds.

Second, even a successful regime change policy might take too long to affect the current nuclear standoff. In fact, it could lead the regime to speed up its nuclear weapons efforts in a bid to gain the immunity it may believe the bomb would provide.

Third, it is not clear that the United States has the tools needed to succeed. At the far ends of regime change policy, Washington could back guerrilla groups such as the ethnic Baluchi Jundallah and seek to create violence within Iran. The question is whether such steps would shorten or lengthen the life of the regime, for terrorist violence—even violence targeted at regime officials—is unlikely to turn the populace against the authorities. The opposition to the regime that is visible, for example, in the June 2009 Green Revolution protests, is based not in ethnic or religious grievances but squarely in the desire for a more open, democratic government that respects human rights.

Fourth, such an American policy might destroy the current anti-Iran coalition and whatever possibility exists for a negotiated solution to the Iran crisis. It is unlikely that Arab allies, the P5+1 (the five permanent members of the UN Security Council and Germany), or the EU would publicly support a regime change policy, and some might find Iran's refusal to negotiate with the United States defensible. Fifth, success might bring a high price: were the United States to overthrow the regime, it might be viewed as responsible for subsequent events in Iran (as happened in Iraq), a far deeper commitment than it seeks.

Would these calculations change in the aftermath of an Israeli or U.S. strike at Iran's nuclear weapons program? Such action would not be aimed at regime change, targeting only nuclear sites rather than those where the regime's leaders live or work. Israel appears to lack the capacity to strike additional targets in any event. An American strike would be far larger if it came, hitting a wider portion of Iran's military infrastructure, and it is possible that Iran's reactions—for example, sinking U.S. naval vessels, hitting American bases in the Gulf region, or attacking American embassies, and thereby killing Americans in large numbers—would lead to further rounds of attack where the United States added "political" targets to its list. That is, in an extended exchange with Iran, something that lasted weeks and involved many American deaths, Washington's "war aims" might grow to include an end to the regime by targeting its leadership. During or in the aftermath of something more like a "war" between the United States and Iran, it is possible to think of a military strategy that included efforts to bring down the regime. Short of such a conflict, and even in the context of a limited strike at Iran's nuclear sites, military moves designed to bring down the regime seem highly unlikely.

These calculations could change, however, if Iran succeeds in acquiring nuclear weapons. If decision-makers believe, as the president has suggested, that containment is impossible, a policy of regime change would have to be reconsidered. The risks just noted would not diminish, but those on the other side of the equation—possession of nuclear weapons by the current Iranian regime—might be deemed even greater.

This does not mean that Washington must think of the Islamic Republic as permanent and avoid any criticism of it, lest the consequences of seeking regime change eventuate. Here it is useful to consider President Ronald Reagan's policy toward the Soviet Union. Reagan believed he was constraining Soviet conduct while presenting the USSR with a military and ideological challenge. He made clear his desire for the demise of the Soviet Union and of communism, but did not engage in direct efforts to subvert the regime in Moscow. On the contrary, Reagan engaged in active diplomacy with its leaders to solve problems amicably. At the same time, his missile defense program, military buildup, and active opposition to the Soviets in the Third World were meant to bring an eventual end to the Soviet regime by forcing them to overspend, degrading the effect of their best weapons, and defeating them in indirect military contests.

The effects of these American efforts in bringing regime change to the USSR were indirect but arguably powerful. The Reagan analogy and the Soviet experience do suggest that one way to hasten the demise of a regime is to blunt its efforts to use foreign and military affairs to cow its own population. In the case of Iran, this suggests that setbacks to its nuclear program, a demonstrable American military domination of the Gulf, and the demise of its ally Bashar al-Assad in Syria might dampen its sense of success and ascendancy. As the Soviet defeat in Afghanistan shook the leadership and the people's faith in it, so reverses in the military and foreign spheres might have a similar impact in Iran.

What Reagan did not use against the USSR were economic sanctions of the sort now being imposed on Iran. In few historical cases can one say that "sanctions brought down the regime," but certainly they were an important part of the overall strategy of isolation, diplomatic and ideological pressure, and real support for the opposition that worked in South Africa and may be working in Burma. Were the United States to adopt a policy of regime change toward Iran, tough economic sanctions would necessarily be part of it, just as they are a central part of the current policy aimed at changing Iran's nuclear activities.

Reagan's approach had a strong ideological element largely lacking today in Washington's approach to Iran. Can the current administration similarly bring the end of the Iranian regime closer by sharply criticizing human rights violations and backing the internal struggle for a more democratic Iran? Here one returns to the question of tools. In the past decade, the United States has spent tens of millions of dollars to promote democracy in Iran. Programs have included support for non-government organizations (NGOs) in Iran and others in the United

States and Europe, public diplomacy aimed at the Iranian population, cultural exchanges, and Voice of America English-language broadcasting as well as Persian-language radio and television. More recently, Washington has attempted to help Iranians break through government censorship of the Internet.

Analysts have been unable to gauge the impact of such efforts. Can they identify capable and popular opposition leaders and activists to support and get significant amounts of assistance to them, without making them even more vulnerable to the regime? And even if they could, would the student groups, intellectuals, or civil society groups that Washington might work with actually have much of an impact in the wider society? Do they have the organization or reach, or would they even if better resourced? Given the lack of information about events on the ground in Iran, the question is whether policymakers know enough to be effective in this type of "retail" effort.

Such programs are supported by Congress under the rubric of democracy promotion rather than regime change. The former term suggests a far more modest goal, simply of helping those in Iran who are working for a more democratic system. If the tools at President Barack Obama's disposal are limited, so are his aspirations. The most recent annual report of the National Endowment for Democracy lists three Iran programs: Civic Education and NGO Strengthening, Freedom of Information, and Human Rights, with a combined total of roughly $1.2 million. These programs, and this amount, will not bring down the regime in Tehran. It is better to view them as efforts to show where U.S. sympathies lie and seek any path to help those in Iran who want help from the United States and share these basic democratic goals.

But Washington has other tools that might better fit a long-term regime change through democracy strategy. If the United States moves from the retail level to a broad challenge to the Islamic Republic, policymakers can ask how to give greater voice to the complaints that most Iranians share. Most Iranians are dissatisfied with their government's performance and worried about international isolation and sanctions because they see shortages in the markets and a decline in their buying power. Many are disillusioned with the *velayat i faqih* system of theocratic rule, especially as it has been distorted in Iran, and those critics include many prestigious religious leaders.

Thus a good argument is to be made that this regime has been a disaster for Iran—holding back its political, economic, and social modernization, isolating it in the world, and preventing it from taking its rightful place by making it an international pariah. The United States rarely makes that argument effectively.

It does not appear that the United States would pay a significant price for tough rhetoric. The conduct of the Islamic Republic in all arenas internal and external responds to many stimuli, as the apparent changes in nuclear weapons activity after the American military deposed Saddam Hussein in 2003 suggest.[2] But those stimuli appear to be economic and military pressures, and potential concrete inducements, rather than speeches—even presidential speeches. The most recent proof of this is Tehran's failure to respond in any positive way to the change in rhetoric that occurred when President Obama succeeded President Bush and began to speak of engagement and a new approach, or in any negative way when Obama's rhetoric toughened in 2011 and 2012. As Ray Takeyh said in 2010, "the Iranian theocracy views engagement with the United States as a threat to its ideological identity."[3] In a sense, then, hotter American rhetoric would come as no surprise to the regime and, fitting neatly into its existing worldview, would be unlikely to result in significant policy changes.

Until now there has been no such hotter rhetoric from the United States, even counting the president's 2012 statement on the holiday of Nowruz and its criticism of an "electronic curtain" of Internet censorship and jamming of satellite television in Iran. The Nowruz message is sent only once a year, and given the limits on its length and on what it is appropriate for a president to say, it is necessarily missing some important elements. A more concerted American effort would repeatedly use broadcasting to stoke dissatisfaction, comparing Iran's situation with more favorable ones in other countries and explaining the costs to Iran's people of the regime's conduct. As in the Soviet case, Washington would use presidential messaging, broadcasting, and international forums to turn the regime into more of a pariah and be sure that the Iranian people are aware of the damage the Islamic Republic is doing to Iran's prestige and international role. In a sense, this is ideological warfare against that regime, and may be the most effective form of regime change effort available to the United States. For even if the regime takes such hostile rhetoric for granted from the Great Satan, the Iranian people may be listening more carefully to what the United States says. Here again the Soviet example is useful: although the regime disliked such rhetoric, it did not see mere speeches as a casus belli or major threat, and indeed the regime was not the immediate target. The target was the people, and over time the steady and relentless delegitimization of the regime had an impact. Ideological warfare is unlikely to elicit a violent response, but it can sap the support for a regime that is increasingly repressive, economically underperforming, and decreasingly able to rally wide public support for its ideological defenses.

The efforts the regime makes to prevent the free flow of information suggest how important such efforts could be. Similarly, the impact of broader and more frequent attacks on the regime's practices and its impact on life in Iran should not be denigrated. This is especially true when the Islamic Republic faces some enormous challenges in the coming years, from the effects of current sanctions and isolation to the looming succession crisis when the supreme leader dies. Moreover, the ideological bases of the entire system are increasingly weak, as the Revolutionary Guards grow in power; the once-powerful clerics become increasingly cogs in a government bureaucracy; and some of the most prestigious remaining grand ayatollahs have made very clear their distaste for the current regime.[4]

Would more money make a difference in the impact of U.S. programs? Spending more would make U.S. sympathies even clearer, might improve the morale of those seeking change in Iran, and could help blow holes in that electronic curtain around Iran. The existence of more voices is likely to reduce the effectiveness of the censorship. Similarly, with regard to documenting human rights abuses in Iran and Iran's support for terrorism, it is reasonable to think that more work and more publicity for it might affect public opinion inside Iran as the full scope of the regime's unlawful conduct became more widely understood.

With respect to broadcasting, however, more funding is not in and of itself the answer; to have a greater impact, the United States will need to solve the many problems that have long plagued Iranian programming. Personnel and leadership turbulence have long been evident, and the targeted messaging one associates with radio broadcasting during the Cold War has too long been missing. It is worth adding that other forms of broadcasting—for example, creating communications platforms for the opposition, perhaps through independent terrestrial and satellite radio stations—should be considered; in the past, for example, with U.S. support for Serbian opposition radio, this was an effective path.

Is this support for regime change? Should that term be used only for direct action against a regime, attempting to bring it to its knees, even by using military means? That narrow definition almost caricatures the concept, forcing us to choose between accepting a regime as legitimate or finding ourselves in the realm of covert wars. But as the Cold War analogies show, the area between those poles is wide. A policy that clearly calls the regime illegitimate and states its desire to see the people of Iran free of it, that assists those opposing it in any sensible way they find useful, and that uses U.S. technological resources to undermine the regime's political and ideological support is also seeking regime change. Washington has pursued neither this approach nor the more aggressive one in recent years.

It is possible that both are beyond Washington's ability to master, equally unlikely to bring down the regime, and able to do as much or more harm as good. The issue is in part that success can be judged only retrospectively: only when a regime is gone can analysts begin the postmortems that explain how exactly the unexpected event happened. The task today is to judge the risks and rewards of various forms of regime change policy against the challenges posed by the Islamic Republic.

Iran with the Bomb

Robert M. Danin

What would it mean for Iran to acquire a nuclear weapon or its component parts and the capacity to assemble one rapidly? This chapter does not advocate allowing such a reality to emerge; instead, it examines the implications of such a development. Iran's acquisition of one or more nuclear weapons, or the capacity to acquire them in short order, would truly herald a "New Middle East." Iran with the bomb would plunge the region into significantly intensified uncertainty. Conceivably, over time, a stable deterrent regime might be established in such a Middle East. But the path toward establishing a new equilibrium would be dangerous, costly, and inherently unstable. The steps that Iran, its neighbors, and indeed the international community would adopt were Iran to acquire nuclear weapons are not predetermined, however.

HOW WOULD IRAN REACT?

It is possible that an Iran that had just acquired nuclear weapons might proceed cautiously, at least overtly. The Iranian leadership might hope to project an image of itself as a responsible new member of the nuclear club. It might not want to provide justification for international efforts to try to roll back its nuclear capability.

Yet it is more likely that an Iran with nuclear weapons would become increasingly assertive diplomatically and economically, attempting, for example, to exert greater leverage over oil production targets and other regional oil producers. Iran might try to manipulate oil prices by threatening the Strait of Hormuz, through which nearly 20 percent of the world's oil supply is shipped, supporting proxies to attack oil facilities in the Persian Gulf, or trying to use its newfound status to play a more aggressive role within the Organization of the Petroleum Exporting Countries (OPEC). Closing the strait could raise oil prices by 50 percent or more. This is but one way an Iran with nuclear weapons could seek to enhance its regional clout and establish its regional preeminence while safeguarding the regime.

Spreading its power and influence into the heart of the Middle East is both a manifestation of Iran's self-defined interest as well as a reflection of its revolutionary ethos. Iran is ideologically oriented toward reshaping the Middle East into its vision of righteousness and has turned anti-Americanism, opposition to Israel, subversion of U.S.-allied Persian Gulf kingdoms, and upending Sunni-dominated Arab states into regional objectives.[1]

Tehran would likely conclude, perhaps mistakenly, that nuclear status had won it a certain degree of protection against outside attack. This, in turn, would give the Iranians greater confidence, again perhaps misplaced, to step up efforts to spread instability abroad, so long as its actions had some degree of deniability. To be sure, the Iranians would not want to provoke an attack. But the regime has proven an ability to act recklessly—the ruthless 1992 and 1994 Buenos Aires bombings and the extraordinary recent plot to assassinate the Saudi ambassador in Washington are just two examples.

Iran could act in a number of other destabilizing ways. Through rhetoric and covert means, it might try to stir up Shiite populations in Iraq, Bahrain, and Saudi Arabia. It would likely seek to strengthen its external nonstate allies—Hezbollah, Islamic Jihad, and possibly Hamas, as well as Iraqi Shia militants and Afghan militants—that allow it to challenge regimes and provide Tehran a degree of deniability. It would also likely press Iraq and Afghanistan to align more closely with Tehran. That Iran would test and probe the limits of the international community's resolve to keep it in check should be expected. The danger, as always, is that Iran would overstep. Iran's proxies may also ratchet up their activities based on a miscalculation that they had a nuclear umbrella that provided them greater freedom to maneuver.

Iran's nuclear capability could lead it to use its conventional military forces more aggressively. Already, Iran has built up its naval forces into the best-equipped, trained, and organized service of the country's military establishment. Iran possesses kilo-class submarines and other platforms that could use Djibouti as a logistical base to support a large and sustained presence in the Gulf of Aden and the Red Sea.[2] Iran might seek to assert itself on the seas, stepping up existing challenges to outside naval activities proximate to Iran's shores while increasing transit of the Suez Canal to expand the range and frequency of Iranian naval activities in the Mediterranean. In this context, the chances increase for a conflict between Iran and its neighbors or even the United States over access to the Strait of Hormuz. A nuclear-armed Iran might calculate that it had more freedom to carry out its periodic threat to close the strait and disrupt oil flows from Saudi Arabia, Kuwait, and the United Arab Emirates (UAE). Were it to do so, the United States and other powers would have to take Iran's nuclear capabilities into consideration in fashioning a response.

A second concern is how Tehran would incorporate its nuclear capability into its defense doctrine. Given Iran's fear of encirclement and sense of constant threat, its leadership might be quick to rely on its nuclear weapons to defend against threats. One could easily imagine a scenario whereby Iran came to believe it would soon be attacked, and therefore decided to move its nuclear forces to alert status. The United States simply does not know, nor perhaps may the Iranians themselves, how the possession of nuclear weapons would affect Iran's overall military conduct. That uncertainty would also be inherently unsettling to Iran's neighbors.

A third critical concern is custody of nuclear weapons. Iran's capacity to safeguard such weapons is unknown. Its command and control mechanisms might be insufficient to prevent either accidental or unauthorized use. Nuclear materials, if not the weapons themselves, might be vulnerable to theft or unauthorized transfers. Iran could also deliberately transfer nuclear materials to terrorist organizations it supports, such as Hezbollah, Hamas, or Islamic Jihad. So far, Iran has not transferred chemical or biological weaponry to these groups, and it is therefore not likely that it would choose to do so with nuclear materials. But it is also possible that Iran could share them with an ally, such as Syria, providing an added deterrent against outside military intervention in that country. Moreover, an Iran reeling from punitive economic sanctions might consider selling its nuclear know-how or weaponry to another country, such as Venezuela.

THE REGIONAL AND INTERNATIONAL REACTION

Many experts debate whether Iran's acquisition of nuclear weapons would provoke its Arab neighbors to move closer to Iran, or to work with one another or an outside power against Iran. In the Middle East, this is frequently a false choice. Iran's neighbors would surely feel more vulnerable and disenchanted with the United States for having failed to deny or destroy Iran's nuclear weapons production capabilities. As such, the pace of diplomatic exchanges between Tehran and Gulf capitals might intensify with a concomitant if superficial improvement in relations. However, this would not prevent Arab leaders from quietly or covertly exploring ways to enhance security ties with Washington, Europe, and even Israel. At the same time, countries in the Middle East, Europe, and elsewhere might move to accommodate the new Iranian reality and attempt to diminish the significance of Iran's having crossed the nuclear weapons threshold.

Iran's nuclear developments could spur other Middle East countries to see how they might acquire nuclear capabilities. Algeria, Bahrain, Egypt, Jordan, Turkey, Saudi Arabia, and the UAE have all expressed a desire to develop nuclear energy programs. Egypt, Turkey, and especially Saudi Arabia would be the leading contenders for intensifying such exploratory efforts. Nonetheless, it takes considerable time and expense to develop nuclear weapons. Egypt, consumed with overwhelming economic and other domestic challenges, probably could not devote the resources necessary to the task. Turkey, as a NATO member, would likely receive inducements to prevent it from seeking its own capacity. Unless one of the existing nuclear weapons states made an outright sale, it would likely take at least a decade for another country in the region to develop nuclear capabilities. Given the immediacy of the challenge, Saudi Arabia would be most likely to seek outside assistance in procuring or purchasing a weapon. Riyadh would be the most motivated to counter the increased Iranian threat, given the Saudi role as the custodian of Islam's two holiest sites, its long-standing rivalry with and proximity to Iran, and its wealth. Prince Turki al-Faisal was unambiguous in saying last year, through a senior official, "We cannot live in a situation where Iran has nuclear weapons and we don't. It's as simple as that."[3] The Saudis could buy nuclear weapons outright from Pakistan or even possibly North Korea. Alternatively, Pakistan might be tempted or induced financially to extend its nuclear deterrent to Saudi Arabia. What is clear is that Iran's acquisition of nuclear weapons would provide an added incentive for other Middle Eastern countries to pursue their own nuclear weapons.[4]

Israel, the Middle East's sole existing nuclear weapons power, views Iran with nuclear weapons as an existential threat. One cannot assume that were Iran to acquire nuclear weapons that a deterrent relationship, based on mutually assured destruction, would automatically develop to prevent either Iran or Israel from striking one another. Israel's immediate reaction to Iran's acquisition of nuclear weapons, like many other states in the region that had relied on the United States to prevent Iran from attaining this status, would be a strong sense of abandonment. Israel would believe that it mistakenly resisted its natural instinct to rely on itself. The impulse to act assertively and unilaterally would then intensify. Israel indeed might attempt to destroy Iran's newly established incipient nuclear arsenal before it expanded and Iran developed a second-strike capability. Israel might also seek to confront aggressive third parties backed by Iran, such as Hamas or Islamic Jihad, both to reestablish its military preeminence and to demonstrate that Iran's bomb would not constrain Israel's freedom to maneuver.

Israel, with its arsenal of perhaps one hundred to two hundred nuclear warheads and a delivery triad, would likely debate altering its long-standing ambiguous declaratory policy. Continuing to adhere to this ambiguity could risk it losing some of the deterrent effect of its nuclear arsenal. Some Israelis would be tempted to bring the bomb out of the basement and acknowledge Israel's nuclear arsenal while spelling out criteria for its use. Such an overt policy would increase pressure on the Arab states to challenge Israel's nuclear status in international forums, and many Arabs might feel forced to publicly warm to Iran as Israel's nuclear opponent.

Iran with the bomb would also have a difficult set of calculations to make with respect to Israel. Even if its intentions in developing the bomb were not primarily offensive but instead were largely aimed at regime preservation, Iran's new strategic situation could lead its leadership to act before being acted upon. Tehran might calculate, rightly or wrongly, that in a crisis Israel would likely strike Iran's newly developed nuclear arsenal, and might therefore use its own weapon first. Meanwhile, feeling vulnerable with a small nuclear arsenal, Iran would likely seek to expand its stockpile and thereby increase its ability to survive an outside effort to destroy it.

An arms race and introduction of more nuclear powers might lead to shifting alliances and increased regional uncertainty. The greater the proliferation, the greater the potential for miscommunication, unclear signaling, and miscalculation. Moreover, as Iran extended the range of its missile arsenal in the years and decades ahead, more countries would come into range of Iran's weapons, including western Europe and possibly the continental United States. This would make balance-of-power calculations all the more complex and potentially unstable.

Iran's nuclearization would be a terrible blow to the Nonproliferation Treaty (NPT) and global counterproliferation efforts. Iran would have exposed the international community's inability or unwillingness to prevent a signatory from demonstrating that it is possible to employ subterfuge in pursuit of nuclear weapons. This would call into question the integrity of the entire NPT regime and the treaty's enforcement mechanisms, to the extent they exist. The demonstration effect would be clear to nuclear aspirants: adhere to the NPT for as long as possible while ostensibly pursuing peaceful nuclear capabilities. If more states in the Middle East were to proliferate, the amount of potentially unsecured nuclear material would increase, presenting a distinct challenge to the United States' professed desire to secure and eventually eliminate the world's nuclear weapons.

IMPLICATIONS FOR THE UNITED STATES

Iran's development of nuclear weapons would constitute a significant setback to the United States and its credibility worldwide. Having led the effort to prevent Iran from acquiring such weapons, the United States would have demonstrably failed. Radical and revisionist forces worldwide would be encouraged by Iran's snubbing of the international community.

To limit this damage to its credibility, the United States would have to move quickly to preserve its predominance in the Strait of Hormuz, shore up its standing among its allies, and strengthen regional stability. The United States should try to take away many of the benefits that Iran might seek to gain from its nuclear program. Isolating Iran further internationally would be critical in countering Tehran's aspirations to become a regional superpower. No single act, short of launching a preventive war against Iran, would reverse the blow. That alone is not a reason to strike. But a wide range of measures would be needed as an alternative.

Consistent with this intent would be a more assertive strategy to limit and roll back Iran's nuclear arsenal. Only a credible and robust U.S. military response to provocative Iranian behavior would have a chance of keeping Tehran in check. This would require sustained military vigilance and continued economic and political confrontation, including intensified economic sanctions, diplomatic isolation, and regional defense alliances. Such a policy would aim to constrain Iran while holding open the prospect of relief should Iran dismantle and destroy its nuclear arsenal. The United States would need to adopt a declaratory policy that left no room for ambiguity regarding Iran's behavior: Iran should be warned that any effort to transfer nuclear weapons, materials, or technology would be considered a casus belli. Washington would need to warn Tehran that using its nuclear weapons against any party, or enabling others to do so, would invite massive retaliation. Iran should also be warned that actions to support terrorists or moves to subvert other states would be met by force. Moreover, Iran must be told that even moving its nuclear forces to alert status could prompt an immediate U.S. military strike. The basic goal would be to deter Iranians from considering using their weapons or transferring their nuclear materials to anyone else.

The size of the arsenal that Iran would develop is important. Instead of conferring an extra layer of protection against foreign attack, a small Iranian nuclear arsenal might actually precipitate a strike against it. There would be a window between the time Iran acquired a weapon or two and when it built enough to ensure its survivability and second-strike capability. During this interval, Iran's weapons or delivery systems—missile launchers, ships, aircraft—would be tempting targets for a surprise attack, even though such a move could easily escalate into a conventional war. Were it possible to guarantee that a covert operation or military strike could be conducted that would not produce nuclear fallout, preventive strikes against Iran's nuclear arsenal would be an option—however unprecedented—that other nuclear powers might wish to consider. As Robert D. Blackwill explains in this volume, were Iran to have one or two nuclear weapons, the United States (as well as Israel) would have an incentive to halt the Iranian nuclear program before Iran developed more or placed those it had in fortified and protected underground facilities, such as Fordow.

In any scenario, Washington would need to shore up its alliances, particularly with countries feeling most vulnerable and suspicious of its enduring commitment. These include Bahrain, Egypt, Jordan, Saudi Arabia, and the UAE. The diminished credibility that the United States would likely enjoy among its allies in the region after Iran were to go nuclear would require the United States to demonstrate its sustained commitment to protecting its allies. To do so, the United

States would need to visibly deploy significantly greater numbers of U.S. naval and air assets to its bases and waterways in the Persian Gulf than exist at present as a symbol of its resolve. Turkey's defense needs should be enhanced within NATO. Addressing legitimate Israeli anxieties would require intensified bilateral engagement. Additional missile defense capabilities should be deployed to the Middle East as part of the new U.S. effort to extend its defense umbrella to the states challenged by Iran. This might require a new regional security architecture, including an expanded role regionally for NATO, to intensify constraints on Iran.

Combined with such an approach might be a more overt public policy of support for regime change. Hence, the United States would deem Tehran's behavior as having demonstrated its unsuitability to possess nuclear weapons. Iran would have to dispense with either its weapons or its existing regime. This does not mean that the United States would declare war on Iran or use violence to topple the Iranian regime. Instead, as Elliott Abrams argues in this volume, the United States would reach out to support the democratic aspirations of the Iranian people, using a wide array of tools, including broadcast and social media, to convey the message that the United States sought a new and more representative Iranian government. American officials would step up their engagement with and possible recognition of Iranian exiles. The United States would then articulate a vision of an Iran that could be a responsible member of the international community.

Because Iran's acquisition of nuclear weapons would place it in even further contravention of the United Nations (UN), immediate Security Council action should in such circumstances be pursued to put Iran on the defensive diplomatically, such as by calling for additional robust sanctions. Potentially this could mean targeting Iranian imports of materials such as refined gasoline and other basic commodities and isolating Iran from further international financial flows.[5] Even if further action at the UN Security Council were stymied, the United States could inflict punishing sanctions unilaterally. This would help attract other allies to take similar steps. To be sure, mobilizing international support for such anti-Iranian efforts might prove to be more difficult given Iran's newfound nuclear strength and the temptation of many states to try to accommodate its new nuclear reality. The UN Security Council might be further paralyzed by Russian and Chinese recalcitrance. But an ad hoc coalition of powerful countries of the other permanent Security Council members, combined with the European Union, could coalesce around such sanctions.

The acquisition of nuclear weapons by other states in the region would be destabilizing, as there could be no guarantees that respective parties would adhere to shared "rules of the road." More nuclear weapons states in the Middle East—especially among countries that don't communicate with or recognize one another—dramatically increases the possibilities for miscalculation and accidental war. Moreover, each additional nuclear weapons state exponentially increases the dangers of nuclear theft, spread of unsecured nuclear materials, or preventive war. Even if the likelihood of such scenarios is relatively low, the lethality of nuclear weapons makes the risk extremely high—and makes the desirability of averting widespread proliferation an imperative.

A critical goal for the United States thus would be to dissuade other states from emulating a nuclear Iran. Extensive use of credible military threats, continuing economic sanctions, and challenging Iran's regional ambitions might dissuade other states that might be considering pursuing nuclear weapons. For those states that would seek their own nuclear arsenals out of fear of Iran's, the United States should reiterate its commitment to countering any hostile act by Iran and defending them from Iranian aggression. Formal security assurances might be warranted. As part of this effort, the United States would need to increase its military-to-military relations with its partners in the region, such as supplying them with more conventional weapons, fortifying basing arrangements, and providing greater missile defense.

Iran with the bomb would drastically change the Middle East. The Iranian regime would likely feel emboldened and be prone to increase its efforts to stir up Shiite populations in the Gulf and trouble elsewhere. Iran might also feel emboldened to exert its influence in other ways, including militarily. However a nuclear Iran would act, its neighbors would feel more vulnerable. The incentive for one of them—especially Israel—to attack Iran before it grew even stronger would only increase. The only way to mitigate these dangers, short of rolling back Iran's nuclear arsenal, would be a sustained and active military, economic, and political strategy led by the United States to deprive the Iranian regime of the perceived benefits of its nuclear status. Rather than withdraw from the Gulf, the emergence of an Iran with nuclear weapons would require that the United States redouble its commitment to countering the Iranian threat.

Conclusion: How to Think About the Iranian Nuclear Problem

Robert D. Blackwill

The purpose of this volume is to provide clarity with respect to various U.S. policy choices regarding the Iranian nuclear weapons programs. Authors have made no effort to persuade readers on behalf of any particular American action. In the context of these earlier analyses, this concluding chapter suggests four broad principles to assist in analyzing the Iranian problem and in coming to informed and wise policy prescriptions.

BE CAREFUL ABOUT HISTORICAL ANALOGIES TO INFLUENCE U.S. POLICY DECISIONS

The U.S. debate on the Iranian nuclear weapons issue and what to do about it is replete with the use of historical analogies.

AGAINST AN ATTACK

- "The first argument, that Iran is too crazy to be deterred, is historically untenable. Stalin's Soviet Union was viewed in exactly the same terms. NSC-68, one of the most famous American intelligence assessments of the Cold War, judged Moscow to be 'animated by a new fanatic faith, antithetical to our own,' aimed at 'domination of the Eurasian landmass.' . . . Stalin and Mao might have been bloodthirsty fanatics, but they were not suicidal. Nor is Mahmoud Ahmadinejad."[1]
- "A U.S. military strike on Iran today should be avoided for the same prudent reasons that led Eisenhower and Kennedy to choose diplomacy and arms control over preventive war in their dealings with the Soviet Union and China."[2]
- "If Tehran did put together a bomb, it might not be deployed. . . . Apartheid-era South Africa, for instance, built a handful of nuclear

weapons, kept them stored unassembled in a vault, and eventually dismantled them. . . . India, for a decade after its first nuclear test, didn't even bother to prepare a bomb. When it eventually did, neither it nor Pakistan meaningfully deployed their weapons for another ten years."[3]

- "Yet history suggests that nukes don't inevitably beget nukes. A declassified American document from 1964, the year China went nuclear, identified over a dozen nations 'with the capacity to go nuclear'—yet only a tiny fraction ever did."[4]

- "We are hearing a new concept these days in discussions about Iran— the zone of immunity. . . . Nations have often believed that they face a closing window to act, and almost always such thinking has led to disaster. The most famous example, of course, was Germany's decision to start what became World War I."[5]

- "The lesson of the 1998 Desert Fox bombings should be kept in mind: While a number of alleged weapons sites were destroyed, the bombings also put an end to the United Nations Special Commission's (UNSCOM) intrusive inspections regime, undermined international support for the sanctions against Iraq, and (by removing a vehicle for diplomatic pressure) helped pave the way to the 2003 invasion."[6]

- "Regular U.S. strikes on North Vietnam over a period of seven years under highly favorable international conditions failed woefully either to convince Hanoi to change its fundamental strategy or substantially degrade the communist war effort. More recently, limited allied air strikes against Iraq in the 1990s didn't force Saddam Hussein's compliance with UN Security Council Resolutions. . . . Large-scale bombing campaigns didn't break support for North Vietnamese or North Korean regimes, or for the German or Japanese governments during World War II. . . . Nothing in Persian history or today's Iran gives reason to think Iran would do anything but rally around the flag of the Islamic Republic when under attack."[7]

FOR AN ATTACK

- "So, Hitler or Mao? Germany or China? We can't know for sure what Tehran represents. We are left, instead, to assess risks. For Jerusalem, the risk of assuming Iran is another China and learning otherwise clearly outweighs the risk of assuming Iran is another Germany and eliminating the threat through military action."[8]

- "Conventional wisdom is that Israel is just posturing and that the ramifications of bombing Iran are so horrific that all the talk about doing it is just that, talk. But rewind seventy-two years. Replace Iran with Nazi Germany. Replace Iran's nuclear threat with the powerful French fleet. Replace Netanyahu with Winston Churchill. . . . And what you have is a nearly identical strategic/tactical challenge."[9]
- "And no matter how isolated, a nuclear Iran is likely to spark a desta-bilizing cascade of proliferation. Despite its own isolation, North Korea shares its nuclear technology. Iran might, too."[10]
- "If all of these targets were successfully destroyed, such a military operation might delay Iran's attainment of a nuclear weapon by a decade or more. After Israel's 1981 Osiraq raid, Saddam Husayn was unable to build a 'basement bomb' over the following decade (although by the time of Operation Desert Storm in 1991, he had come close). Such a lengthy delay might provide enough time for Iran's imperfect political process to produce a new leadership before the existing one could create a bomb surreptitiously."[11]
- "The United States is now trying to walk back a North Korean nuclear program that has matured while the international commu-nity allowed the regime to play for time to build a nuke under the guise of talking. Is the U.S. now repeating these mistakes with Iran?"[12]

All of these historical analogies have one crucial thing in common. They are all deployed on behalf of a strongly held position of advo-cacy, either to attack or not attack Iran. One has the impression that the analogies followed the advocacy, not the other way around. In his pathbreaking 1973 book, *Lessons of the Past*, the late Ernest May looked carefully at four cases in which historical perceptions played a major part in U.S. decision-making: World War II, the early years of the Cold War, Korea in 1950, and Vietnam. In the preface, May wrote, "Fram-ers of foreign policy are often influenced by beliefs about what history teaches or portends. Sometimes, they perceive problems in terms of analogies from the past. Sometimes, they envision the future either as foreshadowed by historical parallels or as following a straight line from what has gone before."[13]

A few pages later, he highlights that "policymakers ordinarily use historical analogies badly. When resorting to an analogy, they tend to seize upon the first that comes to mind. They do not search more widely. Nor do they pause to analyze the case, test its fitness, or even ask in what ways it might be misleading. Seeing a trend running toward the present, they tend to assume that it will continue into the future, not stopping to consider what produced it or why a linear projection might prove to be mistaken."[14]

Proponents and critics alike have not yet found a powerful and convincing historical analogy for Iran that would make their political marketing easier. Nevertheless, both sides use a variety of historical analogies to strengthen their cases with far less caution than May advises. In this respect, May's typically trenchant observation seems relevant: "In the public debate, nobody uses an historical analogy that undermines their argument."

This is not to argue that uses of history have no place in public policy decision-making. They can provide context and nuance regarding a current international challenge and encourage policymakers to think harder about policy options. But too often, the use of historical analogies as instruments of advocacy shuts down debate rather than enriches it. Carefully considered, the complexities of dealing with the Iranian nuclear weapons program have little in common with Germany's decision to start World War I, Chamberlain and Munich, World War II bombing campaigns against Germany and Japan, Stalin and Mao, or apartheid South Africa. It is much better to put such historical analogies aside and instead focus on the principles that follow.

CONCENTRATE ON THE FEASIBILITY OF VARIOUS POLICY OPTIONS

Ernest May and Richard Neustadt in their book *Thinking in Time* make one of their typical seemingly simple but profound judgments and one that today has piercing relevance to Iran: "In managerial terms prudence seems to turn, above all else, on canny judgments about feasibility—about the doability, that is to say, of contemplated courses of action." Neustadt made the same argument in congressional testimony: "Government decisions, action decisions, decisions which accrete into what we call public policy, always involve weighing the desirable against the feasible." May and Neustadt persistently asked, "Will it work? Will it stick? Will it help more than it hurts? If not, what?"[15]

They emphasize that their "purpose is prescriptive; we seek better practice and . . . marginal improvements. 'Usual' practice, we fear, has six ingredients: a plunge toward action; overdependence on fuzzy analogies, whether for advocacy, analysis, or both; inattention to one's own past; failure to think a second time—sometimes a first—about key presumptions; stereotyped suppositions about persons or organizations (stereotypes which could be refined but are not); and little or no effort to see choices as part of any historical sequence."

A U.S. president should systematically take all these factors into account regarding Iran's nuclear programs. It is particularly worth stressing the importance of meticulously examining the presumptions that lie behind various policy options. What has to be true to make a particular policy prescription achievable, enduring, and smart? What has to be true to presume that Iran will not substantially escalate after an American attack? What has to be true to presume that no nuclear proliferation will occur in the Middle East if Iran acquires nuclear weapons capability?

CONSIDER CAREFULLY THE DAY AFTER, THE MONTH AFTER, THE YEAR AFTER, EVEN THE DECADE AFTER

Proponents on both sides of the Iranian nuclear debate often center their attention and analyses on the immediate effects of their policy prescriptions. Advocates of economic sanctions and negotiations usually fail to put a timeline on their policy preferences, a date when these approaches will clearly have failed to stop the Iranian nuclear weapons program in time. They do not address the core question: What then? Would they recommend at that point using military force or rather attempting to address the Iranian nuclear weapons capability through nuclear deterrence? If the latter, what would be the likely reaction over the next decade in Saudi Arabia, Egypt, and Turkey regarding their nuclear options? And how would American power and influence in the region and globally be affected in the years ahead by such a failure of U.S. policy?

Those who favor an attack on Iran in many cases similarly do not carefully evaluate its longer-term implications. What do they forecast as plausible Iranian responses and how would the United States deal with them? What would be the immediate reaction in individual Arab nations? At the United Nations? What would be the consequences for the Middle East Peace Process in the years ahead? How would it affect Tehran's influence in the Middle East writ large, including U.S. policy objectives in Iraq and Afghanistan? How long would the American public support a war with Iran?

These sorts of fundamental questions need to be thoroughly and objectively addressed before decisive policy decisions are made. This was not done before U.S. acquiescence in the 1990s to the North Korean and Pakistani nuclear weapons programs. (Those cases and others arguably demonstrate that not acting can have the same negative strategic consequences as acting in the wrong way.) It was also not done in advance of the 2003 American invasion of Iraq. The corrosive impact of those enduring administration policy lapses regarding U.S. national interests continues to this day and for the foreseeable future. Washington should deal with Iran's nuclear weapons programs with much greater care and foresight.

BEWARE OF UNANTICIPATED CONSEQUENCES OF POLICY ACTIONS

The sociologist Robert K. Merton famously identified five causes of unanticipated consequences:

- *Ignorance.* It is impossible to know everything, to anticipate everything.
- *Error.* Incorrect analysis of the problem or adopting policies that worked in the past may not apply to the current situation.
- *Immediate interest.* This may override long-term interests, "an imperious immediacy of interest" in which policymakers want the intended consequence of an action so much that they purposefully choose to ignore unintended effects.
- *Basic values.* These require or prohibit certain actions, even if the long-term result might be unfavorable.
- *Self-defeating prophecy.* "A false definition of the situation evokes a new behavior which makes the original false conception come true."[16]

Policymakers often fail to consider the possible unintended implications of their actions, and historical examples of Merton's causes of the phenomenon are manifest. The Roosevelt administration never envisaged that the July 1941 U.S. embargo of oil to Japan would critically contribute to Tokyo's decision to attack Pearl Harbor. Moscow in mounting the 1948 and 1949 blockade of Berlin did not anticipate that it would help overcome differences among the French, British, and Americans regarding West Germany; unify German politicians in support of the creation of a West German state; and prompt the entry into NATO of Portugal, Iceland, Italy, Denmark, Norway, and the Benelux countries. And the George W. Bush administration did not foresee that the 2003 U.S. invasion of Iraq would lead to a considerable strengthening of Iranian influence in the Middle East. Could there be unintended negative consequences in individual Arab nations if the United States were to attack Iran? If it does not do so? In the evolution of the American and global economies? In U.S.-Russia relations? In U.S.-China relations? In U.S. domestic politics? Keeping Merton in mind, the imaginations of policymakers should run free regarding possible unintended consequences of American actions toward Iran.

The rigorous application of these four principles will, of course, not guarantee that a U.S. administration will avoid mistakes in dealing with Iran. The chapters in this book demonstrate that there is no simple answer to the Iranian nuclear challenge and, as James Madison once noted, "as long as the reason of man continues fallible, and he is at liberty to exercise it, different opinions will be formed." Our purpose in this volume has been to try to improve the quality of debate, to analyze and illuminate the differing policy prescriptions concerning Tehran's nuclear weapons program, and then to invite readers to make their own judgments regarding the best ways ahead for the United States to deal with the serious dangers emanating from Iran.

Taking into account the principles enumerated, eleven questions should dominate a net assessment and consequent decision of how to deal with the Iranian nuclear weapons challenge:

– Does Iranian possession of an actual or latent nuclear weapons capability threaten U.S. vital national interests and, if so, in what concrete ways?

– What is the current pace of the Iranian nuclear weapons programs and could it be accelerated?

– How solid is the U.S. intelligence community judgment that Iran has or has not decided to acquire a nuclear weapons capability?

- Have all other policy options, including economic sanctions and negotiations, to stop the Iranian nuclear weapons effort been effectively exhausted?

- What should the specific objectives of a U.S. preventive attack against Iran be?

- For how many years would various U.S. attack options of what duration delay Iranian nuclear programs?

- What would be the most likely Iranian reactions to various U.S. attack options, and what measures could the United States take in advance to shape and deal with them?

- How long would such a U.S.-Iran war likely last, and with what potential implications for the United States, its friends and allies, and the international system?

- What would be the strategic consequences for the United States if Iran were to acquire a nuclear weapons capability?

- How should the United States respond in the region and beyond if Iran possesses one or two nuclear weapons?

- How should the United States respond if Tehran seeks to acquire a much larger nuclear arsenal?

Endnotes

INTRODUCTION: WHAT DO WE KNOW?

1. "A.Q. Khan and Onward Proliferation from Pakistan," in *Nuclear Black Markets: Pakistan, A.Q. Khan, and the Rise of Proliferation Networks*, International Institute for Strategic Studies, May 2, 2007, pp. 70–71.
2. Anthony H. Cordesman and Khalid R. Al-Rodhan, "Iranian Nuclear Weapons? The Uncertain Nature of Iran's Nuclear Programs," Center for Strategic and International Studies, working paper, April 12, 2006, pp. 33–36.
3. Ibid, pp. 36–40.
4. James Risen and Mark Mazzetti, "U.S. Agencies See No Move by Iran to Build a Bomb," *New York Times*, February 24, 2012, http://www.nytimes.com/2012/02/25/world/middleeast/us-agencies-see-no-move-by-iran-to-build-a-bomb.html.
5. David Albright, Paul Brannan, Andrea Stricker, Christina Walrond, and Houston Wood, "Preventing Iran from Getting Nuclear Weapons: Constraining Its Future Nuclear Options," Institute for Science and International Security, March 5, 2012, http://isis-online.org/uploads/isis-reports/documents/USIP_Template_5March2012-1.pdf.
6. Olli Heinonen, "The 20 Percent Solution," *Foreign Policy*, January 11, 2012, http://www.foreignpolicy.com/articles/2012/01/11/the 20_percent_solution.
7. Albright et al., "Preventing Iran."
8. Quoted in Ray Takeyh, *Hidden Iran: Paradox and Power in the Islamic Republic* (New York: Times Books, 2006), p. 150, from archconservative newspaper *Keyhan*, February 21, 2006.
9. Farhang-i Ashti, November 30, 2005 (website in Farsi).
10. Islamic Republic News Agency, March 3, 2010 (website in Farsi).

PROSPECTS FOR A NEGOTIATED OUTCOME

1. See Jim Dobbins, "Engaging Iran," in Robin Wright, ed., *The Iran Primer: Power, Politics, and U.S. Policy* (Washington, DC: U.S. Institute of Peace, 2010), pp. 203–5.
2. See Meghan O'Sullivan's essay in this volume.
3. Thomas Erdbrink and Joby Warrick, "Iranian scientist involved in nuclear program killed in Tehran bomb attack," *Washington Post*, January 11, 2012.
4. For a timeline on the covert war against Iran, see Muhammad Sahimi, "Timeline: The Decade-Long Covert War against Iran," *PBS Frontline*, January 15, 2012, http://www.pbs.org/wgbh/pages/frontline/tehranbureau/2012/01/timeline-a-long-covert-conflict.html.
5. Parties agreed to a second round of talks to be held in Baghdad on May 23. See Jay

Solomon and Joe Parkinson, "Iran Agrees to second round of nuclear talks," *Wall Street Journal*, April 14, 2010, http://online.wsj.com/article/SB10001424052702304444604577344021265727702.html.

6. See, for instance, Dennis Ross, "What Could Diplomacy with Iran Produce?" Washington Institute for Near East Policy, April 5, 2012, http://www.washingtoninstitute.org/templateC05.php?CID=3471.

7. This is not entirely far-fetched: it occurred in North Korea from 1994 to 2002.

8. For a list and summary of countries that gave up their nuclear weapons program, see David Graham, "Not-Quite-Nuclear Nations," *Daily Beast*, August 27, 2009, http://www.thedailybeast.com/newsweek/2009/08/27/not-quite-nuclear-nations.html.

ASSESSING ISRAEL'S MILITARY OPTION

1. Nathan Guttman, "Bibi's Purim Message to Obama," *Jewish Daily Forward*, March 5, 2012, http://forward.com/articles/152540/bibis-purim-message-to-obama.

2. Jim Michaels, "Israeli attack on Iran would be complex operation," *USA Today*, February 13, 2012, http://www.usatoday.com/news/world/story/2012-02-13/israel-iran-attack/53083160/1.

3. Amos Yadlin, "Israel's Last Chance to Strike Iran," *New York Times*, March 1, 2012, http://www.nytimes.com/2012/03/01/opinion/israels-last-chance-to-strike-iran.html.

4. Richard Allen Green, "Israel would face challenge in bombing Iran nuclear sites, experts say," CNN.com, March 14, 2012, http://www.cnn.com/2012/03/13/world/meast/israel-iran-attack/index.html.

5. "Israel says Iran's nuclear program soon will be strike-proof," *USA Today*, March 19, 2012, http://www.usatoday.com/news/world/story/2012-03-19/israel-iran-threats/53654670/1.

6. Yadlin, "Israel's Last Chance."

7. David Ignatius, "Is Israel preparing to attack Iran?" *Washington Post*, February 2, 2012, http://www.washingtonpost.com/opinions/is-israel-preparing-to-attack-iran/2012/02/02/gIQANjfTkQ_story.html.

8. Yadlin, "Israel's Last Chance."

9. Gil Hoffman, "Jpost poll: Most Israelis support U.S.-led Iran strike," *Jerusalem Post*, April 29, 2012, http://www.jpost.com/DiplomacyAndPolitics/Article.aspx?id=267955.

10. Jonathan Steele, "Israel asked US for green light to bomb nuclear sites in Iran," *Guardian*, September 25, 2008, http://www.guardian.co.uk/world/2008/sep/25/iran.israelandthepalestinians1.

11. See, for example, Whitney Raas and Austin Long, "Osirak Redux?" *International Security*, vol. 31, no. 4, Spring 2007, pp. 7–33, http://belfercenter.ksg.harvard.edu/files/is3104_pp007-033_raas_long.pdf.

12. Ibid.

13. Matthew Kroenig, "Time to Attack Iran," *Foreign Affairs*, vol. 91, no. 1, January/February 2012, http://www.foreignaffairs.com/articles/136917/matthew-kroenig/time-to-attack-iran.

14. "Targeting Iran's nuclear facilities," *Washington Post*, http://www.washingtonpost.com/world/national-security/hardened-targets/2012/02/28/gIQAjbeDhR_graphic.html.

15. Ibid.

16. Ibid.

17. Quoted in Alon Ben-David, "Paveway III Sale to Bolster Israeli Strike Capability," *Jane's Defence Weekly*, May 4, 2005.
18. "Iran's underground nuclear sites not immune to U.S. bunker-busters, experts say," *Washington Post*, March 1, 2012, http://www.washingtonpost.com/world/national-security/experts-irans-underground-nuclear-sites-not-immune-to-us-bunker-busters/2012/02/24/gIQAzWaghR_story_2.html.
19. Tony Capaccio, "Iran Strike May Set Back Nuke Program at Most 3 Years, U.S. Says," *Business Week*, November 10, 2011, http://www.businessweek.com/news/2011-11-10/iran-strike-may-set-back-nuke-program-at-most-3-years-u-s-says.html.
20. Ronald L. Burgess Jr., "Iran's Military Power: Statement before the Committee on Armed Services, United States Senate," April 14, 2010, http://armed-services.senate.gov/statemnt/2010/04%20April/Burgess%2004-14-10.pdf.
21. "Iran leader: Any attacks bring 'same level' reply," *USA Today*, March 20, 2012, http://www.usatoday.com/news/world/story/2012-03-20/iran-attack-response/53668570/1.

A U.S. ATTACK ON IRAN

1. David E. Sanger, "On Iran, Questions of Detections and Response Divide U.S. and Israel," *New York Times*, March 6, 2012, http://www.nytimes.com/2012/03/07/world/middleeast/on-iran-2-central-questions-divide-us-and-israel.html.
2. Winston Churchill, *My Early Life: 1874–1904* (New York: Touchstone, 1996), p. 232.
3. Quoted in Graham T. Allison and Philip Zelikow, *Essence of Decision: Explaining the Cuban Missile Crisis*, 2nd ed. (Boston: Longman, 1999), p. 49.

REGIME CHANGE

1. Alvin Richman, David B. Nolle, and Elaine El Assal, "Iranian Public Is Not Monolithic," WorldPublicOpinion.org, May 18, 2009, http://www.worldpublicopinion.org/pipa/pdf/may09/IranianPublic_May09_rpt.pdf; Dina Esfandiary, "Why Iranian Public Opinion Is Turning Against the Nuclear Program," *Atlantic*, March 16, 2012, http://www.theatlantic.com/international/archive/2012/03/why-iranian-public-opinion-is-turning-against-the-nuclear-program/254627.
2. National Intelligence Council, "Iran: Nuclear Intentions and Capabilities," National Intelligence Estimate, November 2007, http://www.dni.gov/press_releases/20071203_release.pdf.
3. Helene Cooper, "U.S. Encounters Limits of Iran Engagement Policy," *New York Times*, February 15, 2010, http://www.nytimes.com/2010/02/16/world/middleeast/16engage.html.
4. Arash Aramesh, "Kayhan Lashes Out at Increasing Clerical Opposition to Regime," insideIran.org, June 16, 2010, http://www.insideiran.org/media-analysis/kayhan-lashes-out-at-increasing-clerical-opposition-to-regime.

IRAN WITH THE BOMB

1. James M. Lindsay and Ray Takeyh, "After Iran Gets the Bomb," *Foreign Affairs*, vol. 89, no. 2, March/April 2010, http://www.foreignaffairs.com/articles/66032/james-m-lindsay-and-ray-takeyh/after-iran-gets-the-bomb.
2. W. Jonathan Rue, "Iran's Navy Threatens the Security of the Persian Gulf," *Foreign Affairs* online, October 24, 2011, http://www.foreignaffairs.com/articles/136614/w-jonathan-rue/irans-navy-threatens-the-security-of-the-persian-gulf.
3. Jason Burke, "Riyahd will build nuclear weapons if Iran gets them, Saudi prince warns," *Guardian*, June 29, 2011, http://www.guardian.co.uk/world/2011/jun/29/saudi-build-nuclear-weapons-iran.
4. See Eric S. Edelman, Andrew F. Krepinevich Jr., and Evan Braden Montgomery, "The Dangers of a Nuclear Iran," *Foreign Affairs*, vol. 90, no. 2, January/February 2011, pp. 70–71, http://www.foreignaffairs.com/articles/67162/eric-s-edelman-andrew-f-krepinevich-jr-and-evan-braden-montgomer/the-dangers-of-a-nuclear-iran.
5. See Richard Haass, "Living with a Nuclear Iran," in James N. Miller, Christine Parthemore, and Kurt M. Campbell, eds., *Iran: Assessing U.S. Strategic Options* (Washington, DC: Center for a New American Security, 2008), pp. 111–17, http://www.cnas.org/files/documents/publications/MillerParthemoreCampbell_Iran%20Assessing%20US%20Strategy_Sept08.pdf.

CONCLUSION: HOW TO THINK ABOUT THE IRANIAN NUCLEAR PROBLEM

1. Shashank Joshi, "Nuclear alarmism over Iran is backing us into a corner," *Guardian*, February 21, 2012, http://www.guardian.co.uk/commentisfree/2012/feb/21/nuclear-alarmism-iran.
2. Scott D. Sagan, "How to Keep the Bomb From Iran," *Foreign Affairs*, vol. 85, no. 5, September/October 2006, http://www.foreignaffairs.com/articles/61915/scott-d-sagan/how-to-keep-the-bomb-from-iran.
3. Joshi, "Nuclear alarmism."
4. Ibid.
5. Fareed Zakaria, "How history lessons could deter Iranian aggression," *Washington Post*, February 15, 2012, http://www.washingtonpost.com/opinions/history-could-be-a-deterrent-to-iranian-aggression/2012/02/15/gIQA6UVcGR_story.html.
6. Marc Lynch, *Upheaval: U.S. Policy Toward Iran in a Changing Middle East* (Washington, DC: Center for a New American Security, 2011), p. 21, http://www.cnas.org/files/documents/publications/CNAS_Upheaval_Lynch_2.pdf.
7. Elbridge Colby and Austin Long, "Why Not to Attack Iran," *National Interest*, January 11, 2012, http://nationalinterest.org/commentary/why-not-attack-iran-6352.
8. Lawrence J. Haas, "On Iran, the right lesson is Hitler, not Mao," *Commentator*, February 9, 2012, http://www.thecommentator.com/article/882/on_iran_the_right_lesson_is_hitler_not_mao.
9. Stephen Pizzo, "To Bomb, Not to Bomb, That IS the Question," OpEdNews, February 28, 2012, http://www.opednews.com/articles/To-Bomb-Not-to-Bomb-That-by-Stephen-Pizzo-120228-302.html.

10. Michael Makovsky and Blaise Misztal, "Obama's Iran policy shifts to containment," *Washington Post*, December 9, 2011, http://www.washingtonpost.com/opinions/obamas-iran-policy-shifts-to-containment/2011/12/09/gIQAUD8DjO_story.html.

11. Kenneth M. Pollack, Daniel L. Byman, Martin Indyk, Suzanne Maloney, Michael E. O'Hanlon, and Bruce Riedel, "The Osiraq Option: Airstrikes," in *Which Path to Persia? Options for a New American Strategy Toward Iran* (Washington, DC: Brookings Institution Press, 2009), p. 76.

12. Elise Labbot, "Is Iran Another North Korea?" Security Clearance, CNN.com, February 27, 2012, http://security.blogs.cnn.com/2012/02/27/is-iran-another-north-korea.

13. Ernest R. May, *Lessons of the Past: The Use and Misuse of History in American Foreign Policy* (New York: Oxford University Press, 1973), p. ix.

14. Ibid., p. xi.

15. These views of Ernest May and Richard Neustadt are drawn from Robert D. Blackwill, "Afghanistan and the Uses of History: Insights from Ernest May," speech delivered at the Aspen Strategy Group's Second Annual Ernest May Memorial Lecture, August 2010, http://www.aspeninstitute.org/policy-work/aspen-strategy-group/programs-topic/other-events/afghan-history.

16. Robert K. Merton, "The Unanticipated Consequences of Purposive Social Action," *American Sociological Review*, vol. 1, no. 6, December 1936, pp. 894–96, 898–904.

About the Authors

Elliott Abrams is senior fellow for Middle Eastern studies at the Council on Foreign Relations. He served as a deputy assistant to the president and deputy national security adviser in the George W. Bush administration, where he supervised U.S. policy in the Middle East. Abrams joined the Bush administration as special assistant to the president and senior director of the National Security Council (NSC) for democracy, human rights, and international organizations. From 2002 to 2005, he served as special assistant to the president and senior director of the NSC for Near East and North African affairs. He served as deputy assistant to the president and deputy national security adviser for global democracy strategy from 2005 to 2009. In that capacity he supervised both the Near East and North African affairs and the democracy, human rights, and international organizations directorates of the NSC. Abrams served in the State Department during all eight years of the Reagan administration, first as assistant secretary of state for international organization affairs, then as assistant secretary for human rights and humanitarian affairs, and finally as assistant secretary for inter-American affairs. He holds a BA from Harvard, an MSc from the London School of Economics, and a JD from Harvard Law School.

Robert D. Blackwill is Henry A. Kissinger senior fellow for U.S. foreign policy at the Council on Foreign Relations. As deputy assistant to the president and deputy national security adviser for strategic planning under President George W. Bush, he was responsible for government-wide policy planning to help develop and coordinate the mid- and long-term direction of American foreign policy. He served as presidential envoy to Iraq and was coordinator for U.S. policies regarding Afghanistan and Iran. He went to the National Security Council after serving as the U.S. ambassador to India from 2001 to 2003, and is the recipient of the 2007 Bridge-Builder Award for his role in transforming U.S.-India relations. He was previously the Belfer lecturer in international security at the Harvard Kennedy School. From 1989 to 1990, Blackwill was special assistant to President George H.W. Bush for European and Soviet affairs, during which time he was awarded the Commander's Cross of the Order of Merit by the Federal Republic of Germany for his contribution to German unification. The author and editor of many articles and books on U.S. foreign policy and security, he is on the council of the International Institute for Strategic Studies, a member of the Trilateral Commission and the Aspen Strategy Group, and on the board of Harvard's Belfer Center for Science and International Affairs.

Robert M. Danin is Eni Enrico Mattei senior fellow for Middle East and Africa studies at the Council on Foreign Relations. He headed the Jerusalem mission of the Quartet representative, Tony Blair, from April 2008 until August 2010. A former career State Department official with over twenty years of Middle East experience, Danin previously served as deputy assistant secretary of state for Near Eastern affairs with responsibilities for Israeli-Palestinian issues and Syria, Lebanon, Jordan, and Egypt. He also served at the National Security Council for over three years, first as director for Israeli-Palestinian affairs and the Levant and then as acting senior director for Near East and North African affairs. A recipient of the State Department's Superior Honor Award, Danin has served as a Middle East and Gulf specialist on the secretary of state's policy planning staff, and as a senior Middle East political and military analyst in the Bureau of Intelligence and Research. Prior to joining the State Department, he worked as a Jerusalem-based journalist covering Israeli and Palestinian politics. Danin holds a BA in history from the University of California, Berkeley, an MSFS degree from Georgetown University's School of Foreign Service, and a doctorate in the international relations of the Middle East from St. Antony's College, Oxford University.

Richard A. Falkenrath is Shelby Cullom and Kathryn W. Davis adjunct senior fellow for counterterrorism and homeland security at the Council on Foreign Relations. He also currently serves as principal of the Chertoff Group, LLC. From 2006 to 2010, Falkenrath served as the New York City Police Department's deputy commissioner for counterterrorism, where he strengthened the city's overall effort to prevent, prepare for, and respond to terrorist attacks. Prior to that,

Falkenrath was an analyst at CNN and senior fellow at the Brookings Institution, where he focused on global efforts to combat terrorism and reduce societal "tail risks." From 2001 to 2004, he held several leadership positions within the White House advising the president and his senior team, including director for proliferation strategy within the National Security Council. Falkenrath is founder and coprincipal investigator of the Executive Session on Domestic Preparedness, a consultant to the RAND Corporation, and a member of the Aspen Strategy Group. He also sits on various boards and committees, including the advisory panel to assess domestic response capabilities for terrorism involving weapons of mass destruction (the Gilmore Commission), the director's review committee of the Lawrence Livermore National Laboratory, and the director of Central Intelligence's nonproliferation advisory panel.

Richard N. Haass is president of the Council on Foreign Relations. Until 2003, Dr. Haass was director of policy planning for the Department of State, where he was a principal adviser to Secretary of State Colin Powell on a broad range of foreign policy concerns. Confirmed by the U.S. Senate to hold the rank of ambassador, he served as U.S. coordinator for policy toward the future of Afghanistan and U.S. envoy to the Northern Ireland peace process. He was also special assistant to President George H.W. Bush and senior director for Near East and South Asian affairs on the staff of the National Security Council from 1989 to 1993. Haass is the author or editor of eleven books on American foreign policy, including *War of Necessity, War of Choice: A Memoir of Two Iraq Wars*. He is also the author of one book on management, *The Bureaucratic Entrepreneur: How to Be Effective in Any Unruly Organization*. A Rhodes scholar, he holds a BA from Oberlin College and an MA and a PhD from Oxford University. He has received honorary doctorates from Hamilton College, Franklin & Marshall College, Georgetown University, Oberlin College, and Central College.

Matthew Kroenig is an assistant professor of government at Georgetown University and a Stanton nuclear security fellow at the Council on Foreign Relations. He is the author or editor of several books, including *Exporting the Bomb: Technology Transfer and the Spread of Nuclear Weapons*. His articles have appeared in publications such as the *American Political Science Review, Foreign Affairs, Foreign Policy, International*

Organization, International Security, Journal of Conflict Resolution, Perspectives on Politics, Security Studies, the *New Republic, Wall Street Journal, Washington Post, Washington Quarterly,* and *USA Today.* He has provided commentary on BBC, CNN, C-SPAN, NPR, and many other media outlets. From July 2010 to July 2011, Kroenig was a Council on Foreign Relations international affairs fellow in the Department of Defense, where he worked on Middle East defense policy. Previously, in 2005, he worked as a strategist in the office of the secretary of defense, where he authored the first-ever U.S. government strategy for deterring terrorist networks. For his work, he was awarded the Office of the Secretary of Defense's Award for Outstanding Achievement. He is a term member of the Council on Foreign Relations and co-chair of CFR's Term Member Advisory Committee. The views expressed in Kroenig's chapter are those of the author and do not reflect the official policy or position of the Department of Defense or the U.S. government.

Meghan L. O'Sullivan is an adjunct senior fellow at the Council on Foreign Relations, and also the Jeane Kirkpatrick professor of the practice of international affairs at the John F. Kennedy School at Harvard University. From July 2004 to September 2007, O'Sullivan was special assistant to President George W. Bush and also held the position of deputy national security adviser for Iraq and Afghanistan for the last two years of this tenure. She also worked in policy planning at the State Department and was a fellow at the Brookings Institution. Her publications include *Shrewd Sanctions: Statecraft and State Sponsors of Terrorism* and an edited volume with Richard N. Haass, *Honey and Vinegar: Incentives, Sanctions, and Foreign Policy.* O'Sullivan has been awarded the Defense Department's highest honor for civilians, the Distinguished Public Service Medal, and has three times been awarded the State Department's Superior Honor Award. She is also a foreign affairs columnist for Bloomberg View, a director on the board of TechnoServe, an adviser to Hess Corporation, and a member of the Trilateral Commission and the Aspen Strategy Group. O'Sullivan is also an adviser to Mitt Romney. She holds a BA from Georgetown University and an MSc in economics and a DPhil in politics from Oxford University.

Ray Takeyh is a senior fellow for Middle Eastern studies at the Council on Foreign Relations and an adjunct professor at the Center for Peace and Security Studies at Georgetown University. He recently held the post of senior adviser to the special adviser for the Gulf and Southwest Asia at the U.S. Department of State. He was previously professor of national security studies at the National War College; professor and director of studies at the Near East and South Asia Center, National Defense University; fellow in international security studies at Yale University; and fellow at the Washington Institute for Near East Policy. Takeyh's most recent book is *Guardians of the Revolution: Iran and the World in the Age of the Ayatollahs*. He is the author of a number of previous books including *Hidden Iran: Paradox and Power in the Islamic Republic* and *The Origins of the Eisenhower Doctrine: The US, Britain and Nasser's Egypt, 1953–57*. He has published widely, including articles in *Foreign Affairs, Foreign Policy*, the *National Interest, Survival, World Policy Journal, Washington Quarterly, Orbis, Middle East Journal, Political Science Quarterly*, and *Middle East Policy*. Takeyh earned a doctorate in modern history from Oxford University.

Made in the USA
Charleston, SC
24 August 2012